MYTHS
And
REALITIES
Of
REAL ESTATE
SALES

By Dan D. McGinnis
"The Pumpkin Man"

Finally… a book that provides the truth, and nothing but the truth about real estate sales. **A Simple "HOW TO"** for the real estate salesperson who has a burning desire to excel & succeed in this amazing sales field. . Written by someone who is actually selling real estate NOW and has for more than 25 years.

Cover design by: Charles Tremont, Deviative Design

Photograph on back cover by:
Markow Kent Photography
Phoenix, Arizona

After spending the first 17 years of his life in West Virginia, Dan moved to Denver, Colorado whereupon turning 18, he joined the United States Navy spending much of his four years in California or at sea, including two tours to Vietnam on board a destroyer. After receiving his honorable discharge Dan moved to Denver, Colorado and shortly thereafter relocated his family to Columbus, Ohio where he obtained his real estate license in 1977, while working in a warehouse. Within six months of being licensed, he sold 12 homes working part time. One of his clients suggested he move his family to Phoenix, Arizona where the market was hot and he could become more active in his residential real estate career, which he did.

In 1990 the Commissioner for the Arizona Department of Real Estate approved Dan as a Certified Instructor, teaching renewal credit hours within the industry. Dan is probably more widely well known by his colleagues in the industry as: The Pumpkin Man, creating the first of its kind, the Pumpkin Parade." Dan swells with pride as he dons his custom made ORANGE SUIT and shares that since 1982 he has given away more than 15,000 pumpkins to children in local hospitals and throughout his geographic real estate farm area. Dan has received an enormous amount of media coverage from television, radio and newspaper for his contributions to this worthy cause.

Although he continues to be very active in real estate sales, he really enjoys teaching and speaking to real estate agents around the country, bringing high energy, enthusiasm and motivation to the stage. He says possibly, his highest goal and desire is to help others learn more about how to be a successful real estate "salesperson." This may stem from the fact that his dad and Aunt were teachers for 40 years as wells an Uncle for 30 years.

Dan admits, it hasn't always been easy, as a matter of fact he failed the real estate exam once in Ohio and twice in Arizona, but he is persistent and has a never give up attitude which is why he has been blessed with tremendous success all these years.

Preface

The purpose of this book is to save you time and money if you are considering, or will be considering in the future becoming a Realtor as well as provide you with the opportunity to laugh and enjoy a little humor in the reading. And if you are already a real estate agent, this book will give you some inspiration, ideas and suggestions to help you have more time for the enjoyment of life, hobbies, family, church, golf, or just sitting on the patio and sipping a glass of lemonade or iced tea with your sweetheart without decreasing your income, and perhaps even increasing your income! **Consider this, how often does the opportunity come along where you invest a few dollars (less than $25.00,) and get a return of a few thousand in the next few months, or even weeks!**

I know nothing about the dynamics or technology of flying a 747, taking a scalpel and cutting open someone's chest to clean out the arteries around the heart and putting it all back together successfully. I have flown on a 747 and enjoyed it immensely, also at times been a little afraid. I have been on the receiving side of that triple bypass as well. However to be the pilot in control of all the technologies or the cardiologist delivering the precise angle of a cut into a human being… I just know there is a BIG difference.

Take for instance scoring a touchdown in football and being in the NFL and knowing 70,000 people are watching live, plus a few million also via satellite TV; or sinking a 25 foot putt on the green and thinking of how many people are watching and knowing that this could mean the difference between $1,000,000 in income or $250,000. True, if it is a million you pay more taxes, however which is more… one half of a million net or $125,000 net?

What does each of these tasks have in common? I am not sure because I have never done any of them (not even part time) however, I would suspect they include: confidence, focus, determination, desire, faith in God, and faith in one's self; commitment, courage, pleasure, enjoyment, sense of accomplishment, discipline, practice, consistence, resilience, vision and enthusiasm.

These are issues most of us never think of, yet selling real estate can be as critical, heart warming, stressful, full of surprises and changes, enjoyable, depressing, fun, challenging, as being a successful professional in sports, an airline pilot, or a heart surgeon.

Over the last quarter of century I have heard the statement: "You make a lot of money." "Go make a lot of money" "Realtors make a lot of money" I want to remember and start responding in   with: "What is your definition of *a lot of money*?" Don't you think the doctor who repairs broken hearts, the professional baseball player and the airline pilot make a lot of money? However *what is a lot*? Since you feel we make a *lot of money* would you also like to do the same? All you need is a few hundred dollars, a couple of weeks of school, take a couple tests. And some pretty extensive training.

I will admit there was some luck; God looking down on me, as well as some excitement when I decided to consider real estate one day in Columbus, Ohio. I didn't know anything about real estate. Somewhere in the conversation I was told I could make *a lot of money*, (oh, there's that term again) and it was easy, I never considered the person saying this had never listed or sold a home or earned a commission from it.

I honestly feel it is one of and I repeat *one of* the greatest careers and professions on the face of the earth and a profession where you can make one of the highest degrees of income possible. From a Realtor's perspective if 75% of those who have a real estate licenses would turn them in and move to a different area of service to the public, the profession would have more respect from the public. Let me fine tune that a bit... I mean those who have a license and actually represent a buyer or a seller in a real estate transaction.

Don't get me wrong people I love you, but get some education and training, read books, go to seminars regularly, take some classes, (not just enough to renew your license every two years) go over your paper work, review your input form before you enter the listing into the MLS system and review it after you enter it as well, check for accuracy, ask your broker or office manager to review your purchase contract before you present it, when you represent a buyer, *represent* the buyer. Or when you represent the seller, *represent* the seller. And if it is not in your expertise area, refer it to someone who knows how to handle it.

Myth: You don't get any time off from work. You have to be available 24/ 7 and work 60 – 90 hours per week.

Reality: Wrong. Turn your pager and cell phone over to someone you can trust who has the same values as yourself and *get out of town.* One of the best tips I have received in 25 years as a Realtor came from a very gracious friend and colleague, Dean Selvey. Over the years Dean and I have had some wonderful lunches together. Sometime ago he suggested I consider getting out of town for two or three nights, alone, and plan my next quarter of business, as he does. I have done just that. The first couple of times were so relaxing and peaceful (want a real laugh?) Read on.

I drove to Laughlin NV about five hours northwest of Phoenix, Arizona. First you realize you are away from everyone, and then you start seeing beautiful yucca trees, thousands of them, then your mind starts wandering, racing, and thousands of thoughts and ideas come and go. The one place that is ideal there is the Colorado River, desert golf course, pool and spa at the hotel, and extremely inexpensive rates (if you don't gamble and I don't). Fortunately, while I was there, I never saw anyone I knew.

On my last day after a round of golf, I went to the parking garage, got some sun block from my golf bag in the trunk of my Mercedes Benz and laid my keys in the trunk, & went off to the pool. Of course no one could retrieve my keys & locksmiths tell me they cannot penetrate the mechanisms of a Mercedes. So I spent an extra night at the hotel and had my wife send a key up from Phoenix the next day on a tour bus.

Myth: You work every weekend or at least much of your time on the weekends is spent holding open houses, and showing buyer's homes.

Reality: Consider holding an open house only if the seller wants you to AND you equally want to do so. Never work on Sunday. That is worth repeating. Never work on Sunday. The only exception: if you have a situation where there is an offer to present.

Myth: Show a buyer as many homes as necessary in order to get them to buy from you. Or show them until they buy or die.

Reality: When you go to the doctor, BEFORE you go the receptionist or nurse asks you over the phone what is your problem. Once you manage to see the doctor face to face he asks you AGAIN what you have already been asked twice. They run tests and if it is heart surgery, you end up with three doctors, only one of which does the surgery, and even then he or she has a few other assistants around the operating table.

So, ask questions, ask questions, and ask questions (as Cavett Robert used to say, attorney and co founder of the National Speakers Association.)
If you don't get all of the right answers, "delete," If things go well, make an appointment for them to come to your office. (Doctors don't make house calls anymore and neither should you).

Myth: You are a public servant therefore whatever the seller or buyer ask of you do it.

Reality: The pilot doesn't take off when you want him to, or at the speed you want. He takes off when HE is ready and flies the plane the way he knows is correct and safe. Therefore you ask questions ask questions and ask questions. Then you direct the client into the direction which is practical and best for them.

Myth: You have to negotiate your commission down when other Realtors are being interviewed as well as yourself for a listing.

Reality: Most likely, if you have been in the business a while this one will push your button. And that is ok. After all this book is written to HELP people be more successful in real estate. Don't get me wrong. We are also talking about providing a much higher level of professionalism in this business. I have taken listings at seven percent commission and sold them when the seller had been expired with a Realtor at five percent and it did not sell. Here is a very important question to ask the seller: "What is more important to you, how much money I make, or how much you put in your pocket?" Something you NEED TO KNOW… you can charge a larger fee and net your seller one or two percent more in their pocket when you are good at what you do. Learn how to negotiate on behalf of your client whether they are your seller or your buyer, as well as for yourself.

Myth: Buyers are liar's sellers are worse.

Reality: That statement used to bother me years ago, when I would hear it from other Realtors, and one day I realized, no they are not. "Some Realtors lack knowledge, training and experience. "How would you feel if some of your friends talked about you behind your back?" Sellers and buyers are not educated in our field, and remember if you: ask questions, ask questions and ask questions the truth comes out. Ask them the 4 W's and H questions, and sometimes more than once: What, When, Where, Why & How.

For example: What if we found a home and the price was $10,000 more than you wanted to pay, but you could qualify for it and it was the perfect home? You don't want to move until October, correct? What if we found the home that fit your needs in August, would that pose a problem? Why do you want to wait until fall to own a home?

When we find the right home, are you prepared to move forward with the purchase? DON'T BE AFRAID TO ASK QUESTIONS. When you are asking questions you are in control, you are learning about their needs, goals, and desires and you will save time for your client and yourself.

Myth: Fax your offer to the listing agent in order to have him or her present the offer to their client.

Reality: If you were going to court tomorrow and your attorney called and said: "I have all the paperwork together and I will fax it down to the judge. When we hear something I will call you." How would you feel?
This is no different. Sometimes there could be multiple offers and you don't find it out until the very end. The listing agent may not be as interested as you to get the offer accepted. You know more about your buyer and telling the seller: "Robert & Michele have two children, three and seven years old. He has been employed with the same company for six years, she is a home maker, and they really like your home, especially what you have done with the landscaping and the kitchen. And they are pre approved".
'If you were a seller and a buyer's agent told you that, and there was a second offer and it was faxed to the listing agent, and the listing agent presented it' ... what would be your response?

I have found it common for the listing agent to be a bit on the negative or pessimistic side, doubtful of what you say because it sounds good. And had I not been there we would have received an unnecessary counter offer. Remember. Always tell the truth, never exaggerate.

Myth: Keep your pager and cell phone available 24/7.

Reality: If you had an emergency and needed to reach your doctor, or plumber; do you think you would be able to talk with them within five minutes or even within three to five hours? Probably not. You have a life, you have spiritual needs, and you have a family. You need time away from work. Even if you are single you need time off.

Can you imagine how embarrassing it would be to have your cell phone ring out during prayer in church? Or how about while your friend is putting on the green? Leave those things in the trunk of the car. Discipline yourself to leave your cell phone off, or in the trunk of the car.

If something bad happens you will find out soon enough. Remember where you were on 9/11/01 when the twin towers came down? I was coming up stairs from playing racket ball, it was on TV and a man on the tread mill was telling us about it.

When John F. Kennedy was assassinated I was working in a department store on Sheridan Blvd., in Denver, Colorado and a lady coming to work told me what had happened. When Sadam Hussein was caught, it was announced in church on Sunday morning. Now for the good news! Wouldn't it be great to receive good news three hours after it happens or even the next day?

With honor and respect I dedicate this book to:

The woman who is like no other on the face of the earth, who has stood by me with all my wild and different ideas, pumpkin parades, client appreciation dinner parties where she cooks an entire meal for as many as forty of my past clients to be served in our home. Assisted me in giving away hundreds of pounds of candy and thousands of pumpkins to children, assembled thousands of "Peanut Farm" kits, and worked with me through many other amazing ordeals…. my amazing wife:

Willia Dean McGinnis

Table of Contents

PART I
AVOIDING THE STUMBLING BLOCKS AND PITFALLS

PART II
ALL IN A DAYS WORK

PART III
PERSONAL MARKETING & PROMOTION

PART IV
SELLING THE AMERICAN DREAM

PART I

AVOIDING
THE STUMBLING BLOCKS
AND PITFALLS

This is an important part of the book. Don't let it pull you down, you will find the first two pages a true story, yet, hopefully you will get a laugh out of it toward the end. We then discuss important issues such as mindset, and realize just because someone tells you it didn't work for them, it just might work for you. I then share some actual situations of recent experiences with other real estate agents. We then go into the depressing or down times you will face. Also realizing busy is not a reason, it is an excuse. And the final chapter of part one…what one real estate broker said: "I think this is your best chapter."

Chapter One

If This Is Not For You, Quit Now

Myth: Although you are not enjoying what you are doing, it will get better.

Reality: You should study, review your income versus outgo, your gross versus your net, and if the numbers are not there, find something else to do with your life.

In the 1964 (during the Vietnam War) I joined the U. S. Navy and after basic training and Radio A school in San Diego I was flown to the other side of the world, feeling I would never return to the good ole U. S. A. ever again. It was really a scary feeling. It got even worse when I stepped off that huge military plane at Clark Air Force Base in the Philippines.

As I walked across that field it felt like I was in an oven. Now here I am in the Navy and staying in a transit barracks on an Air Force Base. Almost everyone (except for me and the other sailors) had mosquito net over their bunks. Fortunately the next day we had the privilege of boarding a nice haze gray bus with 12-2 air conditioning. (That's twelve windows on both sides of the bus down to let the hot air flow through.)

We were warmly welcomed on board the destroyer and immediately allowed to help load ammunition and cast off the next morning for Vietnam. After doing this a few times, in and out back and forth, one day the Officer of The Deck announced our ship's barber had stayed ashore at Subic Bay due to illness and was there anyone who knew how to cut hair?

Instantly, I said to my self: "Self this is your opportunity!" I just knew I could cut hair because my mother had cut my hair for the first 17 years of my life, and it seemed so simple. So I responded before anyone of the other 267-crew members & got my new position. Lieutenant Baker was also the supply officer and his responsibilities included all the food, the laundry, ship's store and the barbershop. All Lt Baker asked was: "McGinnis, can you cut hair?" and my response with complete confidence was: "YES SIR."

He gave me the key, to unlock the ship's barbershop and had an announcement made, while we were out at sea and pulling back from the combat zone. This was my second time to ever have a pair of electric clippers in my hand the other time was when I was ten years old and took them out of the box for my mother to use on me.

After successfully cutting hair for four or five of my shipmates, the word got out how those who had received a free haircut from me that it was not satisfactorily done.

One came back to voice his displeasure, and after looking at his head, I could completely understand. You see, I had used the clippers in my right hand. So on the left side I went into the hair, and on the right side I went with the hair. The back looked very nice, however the back and one side was all that got cut properly. I offered to try to switch hands and re cut the right side, but no one was interested!

The ships barber story may seem really FAR OUT but I felt it was humorous, and articulates the concept of sticking to your strengths. Just because you are a stay-at-home mom, or a man who is retired and wants something more to do with the free time you have, instead of considering real estate, why not consider volunteering or donating your time to help others. I am sure there is hundreds of areas you can help people in your community whatever the size of the population.

Looking back over the years, even as far back as over twenty-five years ago, I can recall people whom I had had cross sales with from other real estate companies, or who were in the same office as me and were wonderful people, but they never stayed in the business.

I saw them get divorced I have no idea if it was because they were in real estate working more than 90 hours a week, not qualifying the prospects well enough, not spending enough time with their family, spending more money on advertising than they should have, or they were working every weekend. This is a career where you can mistreat yourself very easily.

There are the thoughts of large amounts of money you can make, like going to a casino, watching the one armed bandits, or the poker table, which are so tempting you actually believe you could spend a quarter and make $5,000. The potential is unlimited.

I have a good friend in Columbus, Ohio. I sold them their first home; they were one of my first five clients. At the time when this happened we both were working in a warehouse, and I really enjoyed what I was doing, driving a fork lift. During that time I was fortunate enough to be introduced to real estate sales. It changed my life more than once as you can tell from reading in this book. However, when I mentioned to my friend he might consider this, it would beat working in the warehouse, he said: "no way." And he was very smart in doing that. We talk from time to time. He and his family have visited us a couple of times at our home in Phoenix, and we have been back to visit them. He currently drives a forklift in a warehouse. My point, real estate sales is not for everyone even if it sounds easy, interesting, exciting and the income is amazing. **If it is not for you QUIT; that does not mean you have failed.**

I know another person who I thought was a great real estate sales person when I met her in the first office I began in 1979 in Phoenix. Just twenty-four months ago, I found out she is about to complete 20 years with the U. S. Postal Service.

Have you ever planned a vacation and were torn between more than one place to go, and on the way realized this might not be the place you really wanted to go but you went anyway, and during that time you kept thinking of the other place and wishing you had gone there. Well there is a big difference in spending a week in one place, and wishing you were in another versus spending five or ten years in a career you are not enjoying.

I know many people who spend the money to go to school and never take the real estate exam, or they go to school, take the exam, take the state exam, and never activate their license, or they do all of that, get a license and never sell one home. **They go on for several months feeling miserable before they decide to change careers. This is actually good, because they did not waste two years, or ten years in the wrong field.**

There is possibly more misconception about a real estate sales career than any other area you could pursue in life to earn money. And it just may be brought on by the public, I meet people all the time, especially people who have known me for a long period of time, and the only way they can think of to start a conversation with me is: "are you selling many of homes?" or "are you making lots of money?" To which my response is how much… money is 'LOTS'" and they response: "I don't know."

The public, our friends and acquaintances especially, see us in a suit, and driving a nice car and they assume we are a success and making anywhere from five to twenty five times as much money as they are. They don't consider the Lexus is leased, or the $700 suit you got at Dillard's is on a credit card. They don't realize you haven't earned any money in thirty to ninety days.

Money isn't everything. I am sure you have heard that statement. And if I made considerably less money than I did 20 years ago, or than I do now, I would still be in residential real estate sales, because it is really fun to help someone accomplish their goal of owning a home, or of selling a home, and realizing they have made more money from this investment than any other investment ever in their life time.

Just to help you a bit more with this decision to become or not to become a Real Estate Salesperson, let me expound. I recently have improved my golf game, with the help of a former real estate client, Mike Edwards, a retired Phoenix firefighter; I watched my score drop by ten strokes, at which point Mike made an interesting comment to me.

He said, "When you are ready to commit to practicing regularly we will work on some other techniques rather than just things to counter your mistakes with your golf game."

Now I really enjoy the game, never a week goes by that someone in my office doesn't stop me and ask if I am playing golf today because I was wearing my outlandish yellow or blue pants and they make joking comments, such as: am I going on the tour?

This then, is a good example for you to look at. I really enjoy golf, however I have not as yet, committed to practicing daily or even once a week other than hitting 45 balls on the range prior to a game, and sometimes I don't even do that. I want to. I schedule it in my calendar and see it written down three or four times a week to practice at 4:00 p.m. or 5:00 p.m. however I just don't do it. I really want to. Still I do not practice as Mike has told me to. Unfortunately, there are a lot of real estate people who think this way too. They don't focus. Most agents don't focus or commit themselves. Make a commitment to the business…Strongly consider this…**Commit or QUIT!**

If your actions and thoughts of your real estate career mimic my thoughts and actions of practicing golf, you might want to look at something else to do even if you do not have a need for income. To succeed in this business you need commitment and consistency.

Unfortunately, I have met many people who took up real estate because they were bored with life, or had too much time on their hands, and they didn't really need the money. To me this is about as ridiculous as eating that dessert after a great meal even though you are full and not in the least bit hungry whatsoever.

If you are considering spending years in a field you do not really enjoy, quit now and realize you only have one life here on earth.

The future belongs to those
Who believe in the Beauty of their
dreams?

Unknown

Chapter Two

YOUR THOUGHTS

No two people are alike on the face of the earth. And one of my special thoughts. I have had all of my life, is just how unique I am. God has given me an awesome blessing, and I am sure others have it as well. That is that the mind just starts working and churning, and creating exciting ideas of things to do to help other people, and generate pleasant surprises for everyone around me.

We hear so much talk about attitude, self-confidence, mindset, faith, and belief in one's self. All of these things and much more are instigated from our thoughts. Have you ever thought about how many thousands of thoughts go through your mind every day? One would think if there are that many, the conscious mind would be more aware of them.

For instance take sports, when I think of the last time I swung a ball bat, or would throw a bowling ball, or sank a twenty foot putt, the thoughts that go through my mind... It is unbelievable. Or as John Denver would have said: "FAR OUT!" Do you realize how much your thoughts have an effect on your successes in life? A strong focus is needed.

In chapter six we will talk about the peaks and valleys of real estate sales, and if you have been in sales any length of time at all, when you hear that statement I think you can instantly relate to bad times and good times, in your sales career. We always seem to be looking for a better way; looking for some secret or key point to improve our sales, income, attitude or our mindset.

If you are anything like me, you have thoughts and many of them every day. Let's just name a few, and see if your mind works like this:

You have two homes in escrow and three listings. With this number you are just a bit below your average, and definitely below the highest you have ever had. You don't have any buyers you are currently working with, you haven't had a sign call, or an out of the blue call from someone such as a past client wanting to sell, or refer someone to you, and the ole brain starts talking to you...

Gee, I wonder if I will get an offer in the next two or three weeks, on the three listings I have. I know all three of my listings are priced right. Well I think they are priced right, well it seems to me they are priced right after all the market has slowed a bit. Oh, I am sure I will get an offer on at least one of the three this week sometime. Well if not an offer, at least I will have a couple of showings, and if not this week well next week for sure!

Now of the two that are in escrow one is past the inspection period, the buyer is pre qualified, so there is no problem with that, and there is a commission check due in two more weeks. Well I think so; after all there don't seem to be any problems. Both the buyer and seller seem quite satisfied and motivated. The seller has agreed to make all the repairs the buyer requested. And sure... I know it's a solid escrow. The appraiser is going out tomorrow morning. I know another agent who used the same appraiser last month and the appraisal came in ten thousand below the purchase price, but I am sure that's not an issue with my escrow, after all, I based the price on an excellent comparative market analysis; the fourth person to look at the property made the offer, so sure, I know the appraisal will be fine.

On the second escrow the buyer is having his home inspection done tomorrow; I know there are several items in need of repair, but the buyer did offer full price. They have their home in escrow and the buyer is paying cash. It is scheduled to close in a week, so they will have to rent back for two weeks waiting to get into my listing; I know they won't be too particular on the repair request. Well at least

I don't think they will. Then of course there is that crack and small leak in the pool, and my seller said they will not fix it even if the buyer asks them to do so. Oh well, that buyer is putting $60,000 down so it's not like they are short of money; if my seller won't fix the pool I would think the buyer would go ahead with the purchase and make the repair themselves after closing.

Wow, the telephone hasn't rung all afternoon that is four hours, well maybe I am just worried about nothing, why don't I just relax go read a book, or go call ten past clients. No, I am definitely not in the right frame of mind, to call past clients with these negative thoughts going through my mind.

I wonder if I should hold one of my three listings open this weekend. No they haven't sold so they are probably overpriced anyway, and I wouldn't want to be confronted by someone coming through my open house feeling it was overpriced, and I am just out to get them.

I think you get the point from these past few paragraphs so I won't continue on so you see, if you have ever had thoughts like this go through your mind, you're probably quite normal.

Our thoughts are constantly coming and going even if not focused on selling real estate; they could be about our health, an illness; it doesn't go away for a week or two, and everyone we know tries to become our primary physician. Believe me I know, I am there right now, day 19 of some kind of illness, saw five doctors, had x-rays of the chest and head, was prescribed three different antibiotics, and everyone who is not a doctor is trying to diagnose my situation.

I don't have enough strength to mow the lawn. I am better than I was a week ago, or at least I am different. This has given me a great deal of time to sit and have a lot of those "THOUGHTS" pass through my mind. Thoughts of the past, the present, and the future.

Will I be ok in three days, or will it take two weeks? Will I lose out on listings or sales because of this time off?

Just a few days ago an idea came to mind, which has really helped me with my thoughts. I began to look at this time of illness as a blessing in disguise, a time to rest, a time to think, a time to add more to my first book, and time to enjoy my home after almost three weeks in which I have been home ninety percent of the time.

KEY POINT. At the end of the day I think of what has happened that was good, great, exciting, & unexpected or pleasant. When the negative or disappointing things come to mind, I block them out immediately, since we want to dwell on the pleasant events of the day.

Then I started counting them on my fingers, because I didn't want to leave any out. I wanted to know how many there were, especially if there were eight instead of only three.

Now that I have done it a few days it has become a HABIT. And I look forward to reviewing the day at evening time. It is quite surprising to me, to recognize just how many positive events there have been. If things are going that well, then there sure is great hope for the future.

So just in case you are having a bit of a rough time in life right now or are possibly experiencing depression, why not give this a try, because for the price, it is a real bargain.

I recently even turned a negative into a positive. Dead on. How about this? I had been expecting a couple to purchase my listing within the last 24 hours;
they wanted their son to buy their home and them purchase ours.

Well she called about an hour ago to say her son wants to save up money for six months before he does anything. I mentioned interest rates would go up before they go down, and it may not benefit him to wait. To which she responded: "I know, I told him that." Then I asked her if she would like to go ahead and purchase our home and have me sell their home to someone else, then help her son find another home in six months. To which she politely said "no."

Guess what! I just realized this is another positive to count on my fingers tonight. Because **at least I now know they are NOT going to purchase** my home, so I will start looking for other buyers, freshen up the listing in the MLS tonight and put other marketing ideas into action. This way I will add another LEAD to my file for a future buyer when they are ready to move forward.

I am sure you are getting ideas from this book that will help you and please consider this one: start counting on your fingers again tonight, to find at least ten positive events of your day.

To Every Disadvantage There Is
A Corresponding Advantage.

Unknown

Chapter Three

What Doesn't Work For Others, Just May Work For You

Myth: There are three agents in your office who sell more than fifty homes a year and/or make more than $200,000 in gross commissions. They never do telephone prospecting or geographical farming; therefore those two ideas are not profitable.

Reality: After research and thinking about what **you enjoy and feel confident with** the most, whether it is open houses, telephone prospecting, or knocking on doors three days a week. Go do it!

In order for you to keep your mind open to opportunities, we wanted to give this chapter the title we have, rather than 'what does work for others may not work for you,' because we don't want you to miss any opportunities for commission checks from $3,000 to $10,000 or more in the coming months, because something you read in this book generated an idea for you. That idea that pops into your head unexpectedly when you are trying to go to sleep or wakes you up at 2:34 a.m. CAN MAKE YOU MONEY. We do not ever want to dampen that opportunity.

The idea that created this chapter comes from an encounter with an associate in my office who makes three or four times as much money as I do. I was curious why he had given me the suggestion of using Power line some three years ago, when he himself later quit using it.

So the title of this chapter will make sense when you read the following statement. That Realtor said he got more sign calls than he could keep up with, and that Power line weakened his income. It did not make sense to me; because it has worked wonders for me. To explain in more detail and for your benefit, here is the situation.

This other Realtor does quite a bit of business with developers and new home subdivisions and has a team of three to five other Realtors working with him. In the past I have made three times less in gross commissions than he, and where he has twenty-five listings I have five. However, with the power line I invested $500 or less and made more than $10,000 each year, for three years a significant benefit directly attributable to the power line.

With this system, when a person calls YOUR 800 number and enters the extension, the system will page you within 10 seconds from the time the person initiated the call. It works 24-7!

The key to the success of this system is to return the call immediately... NOT one hour or four hours later. It is better than a sign call, because you already have their telephone number. In addition it is ideal to make a recording in advance of your listing appointment and demonstrate how it works on your listing appointment. No other Realtor that person interviews will have the marketing tool you have just offered! If you would like additional information about this you can email me at: DanDeeTheRealtor@cox.net. Or call me at 602-570-2442. **This is the best marketing tool I have ever used in my entire real estate career.**

Open houses never have worked well for me, however I have heard other Realtors say that holding an open house picks them up two to three buyers in that three or four hour time frame.

Some real estate agents do not want even one listing; others do not want to work with buyers. To me this is another exciting part of this business and it is for you to determine what area works best for you. Find out what you enjoy the most.

Realtors do geographical farming, as we will discuss in another chapter, blind ad advertising, and non-owner occupied homeowners, either in town or out of state. You should do the research, and not take any one person too serious, since what didn't work for them, or they didn't like, does not mean it won't work for you! It is even possible you will come up with techniques to institute that others have not thought of.

If it is an area like lead generation, also known as telephone prospecting (chapter 18 covers this in detail) and you are comfortable with it, then do it. However, if it is another area, which would actually require you to spend more money, I recommend you set up a budget and determine a goal of how much you wish to spend over whatever period of time, as a goal. Then when you reach that point, and it has <u>not</u> been profitable, STOP.

Unfortunately, I have never heard of a school, a broker, or anyone group who will sit down and counsel with you at the beginning, ask you questions, and allow you to ask them questions, in order for you to determine an area of real estate which might interest you more than another. One more reason that this business is so exciting and unpredictable!

If nothing changes—nothing changes.

Unknown

Chapter Four

Avoid These Costly Mistakes

This is as valuable as the chapter on GOALS. In chapter 12, we will discuss **helping you in obtaining your goals**. There seems to be some sort of destructive mechanism working on real estate sales people that takes away a percentage of their income. Unfortunately, these are (I believe) intelligent registered to vote citizens, who are living in la la land.

Please understand I am not putting anyone down, these are just facts... And the purpose of this chapter is to **help YOU** to not make these mistakes and to help you be more successful in less time. It is as simple as that.

On my way home from church today, Michele Dennerlein, (one of my seller's) called to say a Realtor showed their home yesterday and the buyer told the seller they were very interested, and spent a great deal of time at the showing. Also while I was in church, another Realtor called to say her buyer finally got his act together and was going in to sign an addendum to extend the close of escrow and make his earnest money of $5,000 non-refundable, on the same property! We had been waiting on this decision for a week, and on the suggestion of this buyer's Realtor I had put the home back to active in multiple listing service.

I explained the situation to my sellers as I drove home and asked: "What do you want?" They said well this first potential buyer has caused us to start packing and unpacking and we would like to give the other buyer an opportunity. So I called the Realtor of the buyer who looked the day before and told the agent to go ahead and write an offer. The agent explained the buyer had gone home to *think about it* the previous night. The agent was holding an open house today and would call the buyers to come by the open house if they were interested and they would write an offer. I could not resist, I said: "forget the open house your job is writing offers, not holding open houses" the agent explained to me, they could not ignore the client who was expecting the open house today. Besides she had an ad running for the open house.

Ladies and Gentlemen, you can call the seller and tell them YOU WILL NOT be there! It doesn't matter if you have advertised it. You do not have to be there! We are talking about a buyer who wants to purchase a home and more than a $12,000 commission.

Let me explain to the new agent, first of all NEVER and I mean NEVER let a person tell you they have to *think about it* and go away until the next day. That is a stall or an objection; you MUST not let this happen.

It is just automatic with me, if they like the house & the seller is not home, we sit down there and write the offer on the subject property, or go to a restaurant, buy them lunch and write the offer; or I take them to my office and write the offer. You might want to go back and read these last two paragraphs three more times. **This is where thousands of Realtors let money slip through their hands.**

I am not talking about being a pushy or aggressive sales person; I am talking about doing your job. Closing is another word for it. Helping your buyer or seller attain their goal is another way of wording it.

When you are on a listing appointment and the seller says they want to think about it, ask them what it is they want to think about? And just listen to what they say next, and you will see you need to do more work. Did you know some for sale by owners and some expired listings, interview as many as twenty agents? If you are not going to take the listing, thank them, tell them to have a great life and go home, never expecting to see them again.

When talking with a potential buyer ask questions. If they have someone they are working with, you are not responsible to meet them or let them look at your listing. This is why our system offers a co-broke commission. In other words that means you are giving up 50% of your money so let the other agent do their portion of the work.

If you show a buyer more than ten homes, you are not asking enough questions. It doesn't matter if they are new to town, they think they want west, they think they want north or possibly they want the east part of the city. Show one or two homes in each area, and when you have decided which area they prefer, if they do not want that home, you show them two or three more in the area of town that they want and WRITE THE OFFER!

Next step. Prior to writing the offer, ALWAYS talk with the listing agent to make sure the home is still available. They could have just accepted an offer within the last couple of hours. Make an appointment with the listing agent to present the offer <u>before</u> you have it written. Finally, make sure you are present with the seller and listing agent for presenting the offer. We will talk about this in another chapter. Ladies and Gentlemen, THAT IS YOUR JOB! Computers, the Internet, and fax machines are terrific and have helped us save time, however no manmade contraption will ever replace the capabilities of a human being, which God created? This is **"the forgotten art"; which we will cover in my next book, in early 2005.**

Think and focus strongly while writing the offer, and then review it upon completion, then review it again to see your client has signed, dated and initialed every place necessary.

Where law ends, tyranny begins...
Unknown

Chapter Five

Is My Telephone Plugged In?

If you are currently a licensed Realtor, has there ever been a time when you sort of felt like something might be wrong, sort of like your life just seemed different, like am I really who I am and am I alive and well, or have I died and gone on to heaven and this is a dream?

Three hours pass by and it just seems someone should have called, then your mother or your son calls and you realize the telephone is working; however there are no calls pertaining to your listings, your escrows, and sign calls, not even someone calling to say we want to sell our home, and my neighbor recommended you to us.

Life goes on. There are some good things that happen and some not so good but that is life and that is normal, then it dawns upon you it has been four days and no one has called you to list or sell their home. No real exciting sign calls, and you begin to think. Is this it? Is the store closed? Are we out of business? Then you realize, oh yes, that's right… there's Jim and Chris who have told me to call them May 15th to sell their home, although that is three weeks away. However Chris calls tomorrow and says, oh by the way, we decided not to sell, however we will call you when we do decide in five or ten years.

So what do you do when this happens? It is an ideal time to possibly take off leave town for three days, and while you are gone, don't ever think of the situation we have just discussed in the lines above. Do some planning and schedule the next three months for your business. This includes scheduling time off first of all, taking the children or grandchildren to Disneyland lets say six weeks from now, and prior to that you are going to take three listings and have two sales. You are not sure where it will come from, however you are certain it is going to happen.

Now schedule your time off, lets say Saturday afternoon, all day Sunday and one half of a day on Thursday. Just so we understand each other, lets go over the word: OFF. Time off means you do not write, read or think about real estate, you don't wonder who will call you next to sell, you don't wonder who you will call next and say they are ready to buy, you don't wonder when the telephone will ring again with business. In fact you play like you are neither a licensee, a Realtor, nor a salesperson.

I understand no one Realtor is alike; however I do feel some of us have similar feelings and thoughts to others. My reasoning for this is I have been to seminars for 25 years, where a speaker makes a joke such as: "Have you ever had too much month at the end of the money?" and 237 people out of 1589 laugh. So would you agree of that 237 that 76 of them or 123 of them or even 210 of them were laughing just because it was funny? However, would you also then agree just maybe 110 of the people have been there? So if we have a million people who are members of National Association of Realtors (NAR) could we say 37,000 have had a time when business was slow and they began to wonder…**is this it?!**

Therefore, I feel we have a legitimate subject to discuss, to help that percentage of you who have been there, will be there, or are there NOW! Let's continue then with some things to help you through this process. After all, we don't want to let it get to the point where you have to visit the psychiatrist to see if something is wrong with you, or the dentist for a cleaning because you think you have bad breath.

The idea of taking three days off to plan the next quarter of the year is not a bad idea to do on a regular basis.

In the middle of difficulty lies opportunity.
Albert Einstein

Chapter Six

The Peaks and Valleys

Prior to joining the U S Navy, I lived in Denver, Colorado. From almost anywhere in Denver you could see the snow-capped mountains to the west. Driving west from Denver and Lakewood, Colorado the sight of the peaks was beautiful. Snow-covered Mt. Evans at (14,260ft) above sea level is the highest point in the world you can take an automobile, and where the air is so thin above the timber line, that trees will not grow there. You can actually stand there and look down on airplanes flying beneath you.

If you have never been there, consider a vacation in that great part of these United States.

My point… when you are on top of some of the mountains standing there in the pure white snow, no matter how cold, it is wonderful. However, when you are in the valleys working your way up and looking at the beauty it can be just as nice.

Over the years I have many times heard Realtors, real estate coaches, trainers and speakers talk about the peaks and valleys of the real estate business. The peaks are a description of a great time, however the valleys are a time when business is slow, and things are not going all that well, you are in need of listings, more escrows, or more money, and more clients.

When you are in those valleys in real estate sales (AND YOU WILL BE,) think of the snow-capped mountains, how beautiful they were in the past. Then think of the future when you have so much business you won't have time to realize what it was like when you had little or no business. THOSE PEAKS WILL BE BEAUTIFUL AGAIN.

Sometimes, when thinking back on similar experiences however past, you realize it is your thoughts, mindset & attitude that will carry you through when you face "valley" scenario you realize you faced an even worse situation yet managed to get through it quite well!

Often prayer or meditation or even picking up a couple of great books or CD's to listen to, can be of great help. If you do these things on a regular basis; setting aside daily, time to pray and think, then when those difficult times do come you are familiar with the process of how to rid your mind of negative thoughts, and realize, IT WILL GET BETTER. This might be the perfect place to mention an old proverb: *"Fear and doubt knocked on the door. Faith and courage answered. There was no one there."*

More detail is given in chapter 8 on avoiding negative people. When you are in one of those "valleys" as we call them, you must avoid those people like the plague. Think about it, someone has the flu or is sick with some form of illness that is contagious; you go to great extremes to avoid that person. This time is just like that time. There are vaccines for the flu but, there are no vaccines for the person who dumps bad thoughts on you. You have to handle it. Another realization is there are always more peaks than there are valleys in the real estate business.

Which would be better? To walk across Kansas all your life or across Colorado? If you have ever been to Kansas you drive for hours, it seems like nothing but flat land from one end to the other. With Colorado however, there is flat land, there are mountains, and lakes. Some of the mountains have nothing but rocks because they are so high above the timberline, some have pine trees, and some have snow. The point being you have a variety of views...

When you punch a time clock all your life; granted, at least you know you will have a check each week, or will you? Over the past several years many companies have down sized and people, who have been there for years, are no longer employed where as if you are a real estate sales person you have the excitement every month, every week, or even every day of wondering what blessings will God bring your way?

Will you have a sale or take a listing every week for six or fifteen weeks? Will you take three listings this week? Will you have five of your listings sell this month? Will your income double what last month's was? Will you have a 90% increase in income this year compared to last year? Will you make seven contacts today, and end up with two leads and one listing appointment which ends up selling within a week and get three sign calls from that listing that you turn into sales during the next month? And the people whose home you listed then, will they have you help them find the next home, and since you were so great, they refer four other people during the next twelve months, that all turn into sales and closed escrows.

Thus, your income from one contact turns into $50,000 or $80,000 during the next year. This excitement can help you realize those valleys are part of the process.

The friend you have punching the time clock may not have any valleys like you, however they will also not experience any real peaks, as you will.

There is no security on this earth, there is Only opportunity.

General Douglas Macarthur

Chapter Seven

Busy Is Not A Reason

Myth: I was going to return your call, but I was very busy all day yesterday.

Reality: There were other things I was doing that were more important to me than calling you back... OR, Oops... It completely slipped my mind; I just forgot to handle that one call to you. It is still legal nowadays to be honest and tell the truth when you have made a mistake.

No one is perfect. Well maybe you are almost perfect for a few hours or a couple days and then your mind jumps off track because you are working on over load. Especially if you are doing a number of transactions each year, and your business increases this year compared to last year or month.

You may have an assistant or a closing coordinator. Let me make a suggestion to you about assistants. You will hear: "if you don't have an assistant you are one." There is also another way to evaluate this: "are you paying someone to do something you could do yourself if you only focused your time more?" Then apply that money you are not paying to an assistant to your marketing campaign, take your wife out to dinner, a couple of extra golf games each month, buy your wife a new outfit, or take a vacation.

Now, when it comes to someone telling you they were too busy to call you back or follow up on something, or stage their home so you could start your active marketing (now or in the future,) that comment coming from someone else should cause you to stop and think "Is this person really serious about doing business, or are they not as motivated as I thought they were to sell their home?"

You can ALWAYS work in one more telephone call! Most people use cell phones nowadays and if you don't like to drive and talk on the telephone at the same time, it is simple to punch that one telephone number into your phone and make that return call you promised someone on your way to your car from the office, while you are faxing something, or making copies at the copier. Possibly if you have a hands-free telephone land line or cell phone, you can make that one call as you are organizing things on your desk in preparation to leave for the day.

How about while you are feeding the dog, or bringing in the mail once you arrive home? I agree this may sound like we are taking things to the extreme, however, it will help you jog your thoughts to see where you can get in that extra call or two that you promised, or you feel a need to make.

When you are finally done for the day that is YOUR TIME, NOT A TIME FOR WORKING.

The point is... Busy is an excuse or a polite way to avoid the truth. Learn   to   say: "NO," whether you are the real estate agent and have no interest in working with a particular client, or someone else ask you to go to lunch next Thursday, or to go to a meeting with them tomorrow evening. Say, "No, I appreciate your thinking of me, however I am not interested," and walk away feeling good about it.

I have never been too busy to present an offer on one of my listings. I recall in 1978 one night at 2:00 a.m. I was driving around the outer loop I-270 in Columbus, Ohio on my way home; having worked on three purchase agreements that day, in hopes of having three sales in one day. I went until I was finished. When it means a few thousand dollars to you, you would do the same. Or just as important, if it means your buyer getting the home they really want instead of someone else getting it or your seller gets an acceptable offer on their home. Sometimes you might put in a ten-hour day or even a fourteen-hour day. You could if you wanted, only work six hours the next day or take off three days next week.

Love is not a feeling, it's a behavior.

Unknown

Chapter Eight

Stay Away From Snakes, Bees and Broken Glass

Myth: You can always benefit from everyone you come in contact with.

Reality: In just a couple of minutes you can learn from the conversation this may be a person you want to avoid, because you will not benefit from being associated with them in any way, as a matter of fact, they may make your life more miserable. I am talking about Negative Ned, Debbie Downer, or anyone with the habitual loosers limp.

This is very important; it can put you out of the real estate business in less than ninety days! Everyone has to deal with this at some time or another. It is like a disease or virus. When you are aware of it, you will see it can come from the least expected person. Once you get a bite from it you may want to come back and read this chapter again.

You must stay away from people with negative talk. Agents complaining about high interest rates, bad economy, statements like: buyers are liars, sellers are worse. People, who talk about the bad outcome of a situation that happened yesterday, last week or ten years ago. I know all about this, it seems to be human nature to listen to or create gossip; being around it will cause problems for you.

You avoid bees, snakes and broken glass don't you? This is the best way I know to get your attention and give you an example to show you how much damage a person with negative talk can do to you. Let me give you another example to show you what I mean.

I want you to lay this book down and look down at the floor or the ground, think of something displeasing. We need to get in the correct frame of mind, so you understand let's repeat what to do NOW... lay this book down, and look down at the floor think of something displeasing, unhappy thoughts, something bad that has happened. Now that you are in that position try to smile and feel happy.

Next, hold your shoulders back, (come on do it...it is your money that purchased this book, so get the FULL BENEFIT from it don't cheat yourself) look up at the blue sky, and think pleasant thoughts such as how great it is to be an American, and have a career where you can make more money than the average person. Now put a big smile on your face, or any other totally awesome and apply thoughts you can think of. Now try to feel sad. You can't do it.

You can have a rip roaring week, list three homes, have a sale, and a couple closings, and then spend fifteen minutes with a depressing person, and they can almost have you forgetting about all the success you just experienced. One thing I have learned from this, **YOU CANNOT CHANGE THEM TO THE POSITIVE SIDE! However they can change you, so stay away from them. This is a habit that is just as dangerous as the habit of alcohol or cigarettes.**

You will not find a Realtor selling three million, ten million or fifty million in real estate production per year going around complaining about the weather, the traffic, interest rates, or the economy. For these people when the market is good it is great and when the market is bad it is good.

If you are new in the business or considering getting into real estate sales here's one bit of encouragement. When the market does go down instead of up it is good, because the agents just hanging on by a thread get out of the business. So you pick up on what they are leaving behind. And there are opportunities when the market is weak that are not around when the market is strong.

Additional examples of this slow time, or being in the valley: more foreclosures, people downsizing to something with a lower monthly payment, sometimes even parents or children selling and moving in with their children or parents. When this happens you will hear about it from another Realtor, possibly even in your office, than it is time to get up and go like there is a fire! You can say: "Oh I have an appointment, I have to go" even if you don't, you can have an appointment for doing lead generation, working on marketing items, reviewing your goals, scheduling your week, or reviewing your schedule for the week.

Watch a three-year-old child doing something that appears dangerous to an adult. The child doesn't care because they have not yet been programmed by adults that they can't do something; therefore they think they can do almost anything.

When you get stung by a bee, one way to heal it is to go to the library, find the self-help section and sit and read a book or two for a hour, then check out a couple books to take with you. This works on negative or fearful thoughts as much, as does aspirin on a headache.

Other options: get out some positive quotes, and read them. Let me see, as I am currently on a flight from Nashville to Columbus, Ohio if I can recall a couple from memory? "If you don't like it change it, if you can't change it don't worry about it" "Things come to those who wait but only the things left by those who hustle." "I'm not judged by the number of times I fail but the number of times I succeed and the number of times I succeed is in direct proportion to the number of times I can fail but keep trying." I recall these from a very inspirational trainer, Tom Hopkins. Fortunately I heard him early on in my sales career.

Speaking of Tom Hopkins, here is one of the many exciting stories in my life as a salesman. I was attending a seminar of his in California just a little over a year after we had moved from Columbus, Ohio to Phoenix, Arizona. Mr. Hopkins made a comment to the audience of Realtors that "The Pumpkin Man" was there from Phoenix, Arizona.

Later on during a break, Merlin Blasdel came up to me and talked of how he too gave away several hundred pumpkins in the area as I did where my market place was. Be patient, the story really gets great.

A couple months later Merlin called me in Phoenix and said: "I have a little old lady over here in the Los Angeles area who knows a little old lady there in Phoenix who has five acres of vacant land in Moon Valley she would like to sell, is it worth anything, Dan?"

At the time I knew no more about the value of five acres in Moon Valley than my seven-year-old son. However, I did some research, talked with my broker, met with the lady and listed the property and within a couple weeks one of the son's of the owner of Ping Golf Clubs called me and had me write an offer on the property for my seller. When you experience an event somewhat like this (and you will,) then you begin to realize how awesome this business can be.

 After paying a referral fee to Mr. Blasdel in California and my brokers' portion, my part of the commission was more than $20,000 and during; my first couple of years in real estate 25 years ago, that was a good sized piece of change.

It is successes like this that you can run through your mind when that broken glass, bee or snake gets around you.

You would be just as safe to drive from San Diego to Phoenix with no spare tire, and starting with only one third of a tank of gasoline, as you would to spend an hour with a person pouring negative comments all over you. You have to have control and be able to get away from these people without feeling bad and thinking you have offended them, otherwise all the sales training and ideas you've had will be far less effective.

I have spoken with people, who when I mention the self-help section of a bookstore or library, asked what I meant. Just in case you are not absolutely certain yourself, let me give you just a few names of authors of books that can help soothe the pain of the snake, the bee or broken glass. One that comes to mind right up front is... THE BIBLE, Other authors: Anthony Robbins, Zig Ziglar, Norman Vincent Peale, Dale Carnegie, Tom Peters, Charles Givens, Jack Canfield, Mark Victor Hansen, Tom Hopkins, Steven Scott, Dexter Yeager, Shad Helmstetter, W. Clement Stone, Dr Wayne Dyer, Les Brown and Harvey Mackay just to name a few.

It is always excellent to carry a first aid kit. Now consider this: carry a book by one of the aforementioned authors in your car, have a couple in your office, and when you find yourself waiting in line to buy a ticket, or waiting in line ten minutes at the post office, reading a page or two will be more beneficial than listening to a person with a litancy of complaints about the weather and the fact it is 112 degrees in Phoenix. That person has no doubt lived in Phoenix for the past ten years and has no intention of ever considering moving somewhere else where it is cooler.

One unique thing about this type of bee you don't have to initiate the conversation; they can just walk up to a complete stranger and start dumping. At least with the little yellow insect with wings, he doesn't sting you until you initiate the event.

Twist the optimist and pessimist, the difference is droll: The optimist sees the doughnut But the pessimist sees the hole.
Mc Landburg Wilson

PART II

ALL IN A DAYS WORK

Here we talk about the basics, Just as our parents taught us how to dress and how to make a great impression, we ask would you be willing to do this until you see positive results. Next… goals, make a list, write them down, and revise them regularly, this is extremely important. Then follow up. This is a critical topic. It can help give you a 90% increase in business or more. However, watch the fine line between persistence and pushy, and recognize there are times to work, but always include: laughter, play and a time to cry, for a balanced life. Then, although we have flashbacks with each new transaction as to something bad or good that happened in the past with another deal… learn to experience far out, happiness, unstoppable excitement, at whatever you do, and understand it doesn't get any better than this.

Chapter Nine

WHEN AND HOW YOU WORK

Myth: Real estate sales are easy and you make a lot of money.

Reality: Real estate sales require selling skills, people skills, patience, a strong focus, consistency, goal setting and a strong discipline of your time. I have spoken with people who had a real estate license for more than 20 years and those who never lasted to complete the school course. Those of over 20 years seem to have "just do it" mindset, or "all my business comes from former clients." Well, that sounds great; however what do you do those first few years until you have those former clients to call you?

There are those who have difficulties coping with other Realtors continuingly offering a much lower commission rate, and I have an answer for that one. If you are known as the best cardiologist or brain surgeon in the city in which you live, whether the population is 20,000 or three million, I believe anyone coming to see you, who has the money, and good health insurance will not question your fee, nor will they talk to three or four other heart surgeons.

Consider if you sell 20 homes or 60 homes or 100 homes in twelve months and lose out on one or two because another Realtor offered to work for 30% to 65% less commission, does it really matter? Did you really lose? I DON'T THINK SO!

Want to know one of the greatest feelings to have as a Realtor? You go list a home, and your fee is equivalent to that of most Realtors or possibly a little more. They are grateful and compliment you weekly for your communicating with them and doing your job. The house sells and successfully closes escrow; they write you a nice letter thanking you, and within the next six months they refer two other clients whom you are fortunate enough to assist with their needs buyer or seller, and you move on. It's a great feeling!

Money isn't everything. Say I make $100.00 per hour and a colleague of mine makes $250.00 per hour. And I work 45 hours a week, guess what... I take off six weeks during the year and am happy. I spend time with my family, play golf, and attend worship service twice a week. For my colleague who works 90 hours a week, life is ok only some of the time.

So which of the two previous situations is better? First of all my colleague is working twice as much time as I am so that cuts his or her income back to $125.00 per hour. Interesting how the math works.

Myth: You have to work a lot of evenings and weekends.

Reality: In more than 25 years as a Realtor in Columbus, Ohio, and Phoenix, Arizona I have held a total of less than 40 open houses. It is more difficult to show homes in the dark than in daylight. Bats can see in the dark, people can't. So in business out west, or east of the Mississippi River it doesn't matter. You do NOT have to work a lot of weekends and evenings.

Myth: This is a professional business and you can't mix business with pleasure. This is serious stuff.

Reality: I recall my first closed transaction. It was in Columbus Ohio, Paul and Jo Lawson were buying their first home. We looked at four or five homes to find the perfect one. There was a cute little twelve inch or smaller TV sitting on the bar, and Jo said: "Will they leave that?" I suggested we not cloud the offer by asking for the small TV, however, after closing I bought one, wrote their name on the box and put my home address on the box, and went over to their home and said: "I don't understand; this box was delivered today to our home, but it has your name on it." Jo looked puzzled and didn't understand either, I said, "well it has your name on it so I guess it's--yours. Go ahead and open it." She picked up a ten-inch butcher knife and raised it to eye level whereupon   I suggested there might be something fragile, and I wouldn't use that knife to open it. Ladies and gentlemen, that moment was priceless; it took a few seconds for her to realize I got the TV for them. Twenty-five years later, and still friends, they themselves have reminded me of the story on several occasions.

Myth: Selling real estate is a safe business and physical harm never comes to you.

Reality: Mr. & Mrs. Behun called and asked for the Pumpkin Man to sell their home. I suggested a price of around $105,000 to which John responded: "no way, it isn't worth more than $98,000." I suggested one more time, I felt we could get a higher price, and then honored my client's request.

The next evening I received a call from my POWER LINE. Christy Edwards was looking for her son, Ryan Ridgeway, and his wife who had just got out of the Navy.

Because I knew it would sell quickly I suggested we look at the Behun's home the next morning, and in order for the son to see it prior to work it was necessary to meet at 5:30 a.m. due to the buyer's work schedule. I called John and Bertha to say I would like to show the home at 5:30 a.m. the next morning. It was set: tomorrow was going to be a great day.

The next morning around 5:15 a.m., I tripped over my own two feet, fell on our white kitchen tile floor and it hurt as if I were a two year old. Nothing happened, I couldn't believe I could hurt that much and no blood. Then it happened, pouring out like water from a faucet, I screamed for my wife as I was on my hands and knees on the kitchen floor. "Help me, get me a towel and ice, you will need to drive the car for the showing of the home" and her response was: "you can't show a home now." My polite response to my wife was: "Shut up and drive the car." (If you are fortunate enough to have a spouse as great as mine you are well blessed).

The buyer came back after work and we wrote the offer, obtained the necessary signatures, and handled all the documentation and closed the transaction a few weeks later. That lady (mother of the buyer) and her husband became a client as a buyer and as a seller about three years later, and, as you read in Chapter One, he is helping me improve my golf game.

Somewhere in the past I recall a statement from someone: "When you work; work hard, when you play; play hard." Let's take a closer look at that statement. This is my interpretation of what it says: "When you are working, do nothing else, no playing around, don't let your mind wander off to what you are going to do tomorrow or later today, or what your golf score was yesterday. The same when you are playing: "Don't be thinking about the listing you didn't get, the listing you hope to get tomorrow, or how things are coming along on the seven transactions you have in escrow."

As an example of a typical day, you may play racket ball from 6:45 a.m. to 7:45 a.m. and at 8:20 a.m. you are in your office reviewing the events for the day, clearing up some administrative issues, talking with your closing coordinator and at 9:15 a.m. you begin your lead generation. Strongly consider turning off your cell phone, putting away your pager or ignoring it, and do not answer your landline telephone in your office.

For the next forty-five minutes to one hour you have a goal to talk to five or ten new people; you decide what works for you. I will even give you the words that have worked great for me: "Hi, Joan;? this is Dan McGinnis; I hope I caught you at a half way decent time; I am a Realtor; with TJH Realty and I was calling; to see; if you folks; had possibly; thought of; selling your home?" **Notice the semi-colons**

(not comma's) that separate the words. Remember to pause, go slow, that is very important!

Would you like to know why? Remember the last telephone call you received, or someone at the door selling something? They talked so fast you couldn't understand them and five seconds after they said their name you had already forgotten their name. Here is an example of how that sounds:

A young person, or adult comes to your door & the conversation goes something like this: "Hisir mynameisAndrew, and I'mraisingmoneyforourscouttrooptogotocampinJuly" Hopefully I have got your attention with this example. I am not picking on young people, adults are just as bad.

What works best for me, when I get a lead, is as soon as I hang up the telephone, I stop, take about three minutes to write out a thank you note, log down notes about their personal situation on a lead form prior to going back to the next call. Those ten contacts can be made usually well within less than an hour, unless you allow interruptions. And if you choose this as one of your ways of working in real estate you might consider starting out with only five contacts a day for the first couple of months. Please realize this is extremely important, five a day six days a week does not equal 29 contacts. It equals 30 contacts. It equals 30 contacts this week, the second week of the month as well as the third and fourth week of the month.

Think of it this way, a professional athlete doesn't let the audience affect his or her concentration. And a couple of interruptions can cause your lead generation time to grow from less than one hour to more than three hours, before you realize it.

At 10:15 a.m. you begin your lead follow up, calling leads you have generated who are considering buying or selling, also you might call three to five former clients or sphere of influence, and let's say this process takes until 11:30 a.m. That is an example of working when you work.

If you are new in the business this can be very exciting because you call everyone you know tell them you are in the real estate business, and ask if they are thinking of selling or buying, and **I do mean everyone you know.** I remember when I first got my license in Ohio, it was so exciting to call everyone I knew to tell them, and ask that question.

Thursday afternoon you play golf, at 11:30 a.m. you arrive at the course, sign in, pay your green fees, hit some practice balls, practice putting, until 12:15 p.m. and tee off at 12:37 p.m. thinking only of golf. Thinking on that first shot, where you want the ball to land, how you want to stand, how you want your swing to go. When the thought of real estate comes to mind block it out, and get back to playing hard while you play. Focus on what is at hand.

When you sit down and relax at the end of the day or the beginning of a new morning or the end of the week, and realize you took four strokes of your golf score the last time compared to the game before, that you generated three new leads this week, and took two listings that are priced to sell, and had one buyer sale, you have an awesome appreciation of your life and business.

BEGIN - - the rest is EASY

Bob Stephens

Chapter Ten

MAKING GREAT IMPRESSIONS ALWAYS WORK

Myth: Things have changed, you don't need to wear a suit and tie anymore.

Reality: The way you dress, what you say, and how you say it, mean everything.

It doesn't matter if you are working with a new client, a person from your geographical farm who has known you for three years, a sign call, or your next-door neighbor. The way you dress carries a strong impression.

Over the years clients have commented on how I dress and will say, "You don't have to dress up for me!"

That brings me to my primary care physician, Dr Thomas Schimke. This man stands tall, has a pair of dress shoes that are well polished and which make a great impression, wears extremely nice dress trousers, has on, a starched white shirt and neck tie, and over that a doctors' coat; one of those long white coats, very few wear anymore with his name embroidered on it. The coat is buttoned up. This appearance makes a statement: "I am professional, educated, and knowledgeable in my field of expertise."

Want some more? Now I go and see another doctor who has on docker pants I would guess to be more than one year old, a plaid shirt and casual shoes. When I see this doctor he makes Dr. Schimke look even better than before.

When I look back on my life I ask myself: "when did I become this way?" Was it from my experience in the United States Navy?" "Was it my first real estate broker, Tom Young in Columbus, Ohio who told me to go buy a $300 three piece suit in 1979?" Well each of those come to mind however, I have always since I was a child, been conscious of how I look, and how I am dressed.

Your type of dress doesn't always get you the listing, however it ranks right up there with oxygen. It is important to display self-confidence and other traits however physical and personal appearances, play a very important part in business.

Think about it. Take a look around the next couple of days at others in our profession. Look at their shoes. Let's do a complete break down for men. Have you ever seen a well-dressed man, and noticed his shoes are dusty or, and look as though he had been walking in mud? How about that tie, is it straight and at the neck showing nothing but tie.

Are both buttons on each sleeve buttoned? Is there a neat appearance as far as a hair cut? Are his fingernails trimmed? Take a very close look at the next ten men you meet in your office, Realtors from other offices, the loan officer you work with, or the escrow officer.

If you want to see a great example of what I am talking about, how are the officers dressed on the television series JAG? Look at the secret service men protecting the president of the United States. They work for and serve George W. Bush, currently our nation's leader and the most powerful man on the face of the earth. If you can show the same respect for people you work for as the secret service displays for the President of The United States, you are portraying some respect.

Now let's go back to what you do. You work for and serve a buyer or a seller. There is no difference.

Every time you go out to meet with a person ALWAYS be sure you are looking almost perfect. No little half-inch thread sticking out from a button on your chest or sleeve.

Polish each pair of shoes at least every third time you wear that pair. Take your shoe brush and brush off the dust after you have worn them. These little tips will make a tremendous difference in your appearance. Please don't take it personally, I am sure you are quite knowledgeable on maintaining personal appearance; keep in mind you are not the only Realtor who will read this book.

People judge other people or have opinions of other people based upon how they are dressed, and when you think about it, most likely you have done the same with someone you have employed. I am not saying it is wrong; it is just the way most of us are.

Some things never change, and dress attire is one of them. Aim high when it comes to your attire. It speaks volumes. I have heard of casual Friday, I suppose that is ok, I have even had a casual Tuesday or a casual Thursday if I am playing golf, and not meeting with any clients.

Your appearance ranks up there with punctuality. I am of the opinion that you as a Realtor, should **NEVER BE ONE MINUTE LATE.** If you are going to be late, call in advance. I assume you are ALWAYS on time for your doctor or dentist appointments, so pay the same respect to your potential clients (if you want them to become clients and or remain as clients.)

When you call twenty minutes before your 2:15 appointment and say you will be three to six minutes late, they may not like that, however they will appreciate it much more than the person who shows up five minutes late without calling. **You will stand out and it will make a statement about you!**

Leave enthusiastic messages on voice mails And answering machines. (Incoming & Outgoing)

DanMcGinnis

Chapter Eleven

Would You Be Willing to_____ Just for One Week

Myth: Some people have all the luck.

Reality: You can have some of that luck also, simply by being willing to: _____ for one week. (You decide what that ____ is you are willing to do.)

Look at a professional football team or even college or high school; let's look at the team however that came in first place last season, and if you prefer we can even look at the team that came in second, or even third place.

The team receiving the ball on the initial kick-off had a plan to catch the ball and run all the way to the other end of the field. When they got tackled, they then had a goal in mind to run to the other end of the field again, whether they made it two yards or forty-seven yards, they were willing to try again to reach the other end of the field.

The first team to score was willing to keep playing the game until they scored again. After the team won the game, they were willing to practice daily, in order to hopefully win the next game.

Golf has become a more popular sport because of Tiger Woods. How many thousands of young children have taken up the game that are of African American descent, and how many millions of dollars have been spent by those new people entering the world of golf just because some 21-year-old African American became famous and won many tournaments? He started out at the age of three years, or younger. He and his father were committed to his success and because of that commitment he has set new standards.

Would you be willing to make five telephone calls (cold calls, or FSBO's or expired listings) every day for five or six days? That doesn't really seem all that difficult does it? Before you do that, plan, study, and read chapter 18. Chapters 8 and 12 will create a great amount of power to succeed with this process. In order to begin with the very first contact the proper way, you will have prepared and have some idea of just what to do, & how to accept that blast in the ear such as: "if this is the way you do business you sure are working at it the wrong way" or "where did you get my telephone number?" or "don't you know I am on the do not call list?!"

Understand the football team has done some practicing prior to running out on that field in front of 70,000 people, and a few more million watching on television. So prepare yourself... if you are willing to _____ for one week. If this is starting to sound really exciting, let me tell you there is more to it. If you are willing to call five people five or six days for a week, and mentally prepare yourself prior to doing that, you are on your way toward a very rewarding career.

Now are you willing to _____ for a month, now for three months and now for six months and are you willing to continue _____ for twelve months? If you make a commitment to this and do it, depending on your goals you can have a very rich career in selling real estate. Depending on your desires, and the goals you have in life you could easily retire within ten years.

By the way, for some reason I do not like that word retire. So let's just say you would not have to work unless you wanted to if you followed that scenario for ten years.

I don't know about other Realtors, but for some reason, it seemed after the first few years I always had someone come along every week, sometimes several times wanting me to change my marketing, & try something new. At that point I was ready to say to them: "I have tried to satisfy everyone and it is impossible, so I have decided to satisfy myself, I appreciate your interest, good luck and have a great day."

I get emails every day offering me the magic solution. The one tool or marketing technique or seminar that will solve all my problems, make me all the money you could ever need. Learn to walk away from these so called solutions. That is the purpose of this book, to help you to grow & distinguish what you really need to learn and what you don't.

If you try every third idea that comes your way you will never have time to list and sell real estate. I sometimes feel there are more people trying to help, train, and teach me as a Realtor than there are Realtors. And according to the National Association of Realtors there are one million of us. One interesting comment my broker recently told me, and you might keep this in mind for future reference: Those who are teaching are teaching because they don't know how to sell. Ouch boy...I hope I didn't offend (including myself) anyone with that comment.

Find something, even if it's not any of the ideas in this book, and begin using them this week, and if they don't work adjust what you are doing, and if after a designated amount of time, it is not working...Change.

I followed a program for nearly seven years and the results were not increasing my production or income. Maybe I should have changed sooner, however, I look at it this way, that was the wrong thing for me, and I know it now, because I stuck with it for seven years. Under the instructions of my new coach, I am now above the income target of those previous seven years, where I always fell $50,000 short of my goals.

A few years ago I struggled for a 25% increase in income and never got close to it, and now I am on track for an approximately 90% or more, increase in income for a 12-month period. What is so unique about this increase is that I have dreamt and thought about it for almost 10 years.

The purpose of this book is two-fold. (1) To accomplish the goal of becoming an author, speaker & mentor. (2) And helping others who are real estate agents or perhaps considering real estate as a career, not to make the mistakes I have made or NOT made.

I am extremely fortunate that I look at this business as providing a service to help people, and I really enjoy it! Whereas I have known and met hundreds of people who complain and often display attitudes of total dislike in working through some of the issues involved in a real estate transaction. **WATCH OUT... there are bees, snakes and broken glass with real estate licenses.**
(That is... some real estate agents have a negative attitude and can dump on you with their problems, complaints, you got to watch out for ole Negative Ned or Debbie Downer)

The one thing that separates winners from losers is, winners take action!

Anthony Robbins

Chapter Twelve

GOALS... A Key Chapter

Myth: Goals are just another word for dreams and seldom come about.

Reality: **Matthew 21:22 "And whatever things you ask in prayer, <u>believing</u>, <u>you will receive</u>."** If you set short-term goals (three days or three months) or long-term, one year, five years, & longer; focus on them, put them in writing, think about them every week, then every day, you will attain your goals. It just may take a little longer in time than what you had planned.

This will definitely be one of my favorite chapters. GOALS have been around forever, perhaps some people have another name for them. Can we say (without offending anyone) **'God' had a goal when he created the Heavens and the earth?** And when God told Noah to build the ark, Noah's goal was precisely that... to build the ark as God had instructed.

If you are considering a real estate career and haven't done your schooling and testing hopefully this book will assist you not only in making the decision to go forward with that process, but it will also help you become a success. Just in case this is where you are, let's take a quick look at the process in dealing with "GOALS" for you. First of all you have a goal to become a licensed real estate agent. Next are several little goals, in order to become a Realtor. There is the goal to pass the state exam, then the school exam and graduate from school. Your first goal however, is to attend each and every class and do your homework!

For those of you who are already licensed, I hope you have goals in place, and if you do, possibly it is time to reevaluate, revise, and update them. Or possibly it is time to set new goals. If that is the case, STOP... pick up a pad of paper <u>right now</u> while the idea is going through your mind, and as you read along through this chapter, be prepared to write, as we plan to assist you in generating larger goals. Stretch your mind a bit; if you set a goal to sell ten homes this year, why not change it to fifteen? If your goal is to sell 40 homes this year, how about raising that bar to 45 or even 50 in the next twelve months? If you have a goal to gross $60,000 in the next year, why not up that to $95,000?

Your goal may be to remove all of your debt. If so you need a date. Is that date six months, eighteen months or two years away. Possibly a goal to pay off your mortgage on your home. I have goals running through my head every day. I realize I am unique, AND **you are unique also.** When those goals or ideas pop into your head, be ready to get some paper and pen and get them in writing.

Goals to read X number of books in a year. To improve your golf score by X amount of strokes. Number of listings you will take in the next ninety days. Number of contacts you will make in the next thirty days (be careful on this one.) **A very important key to the contacts is consistency!** It needs to be five or six days a week and for the next six or eighteen months. However when you see your business growing and it is because of this, you must remember to keep doing it, remember this is where that business is coming from and if you stop, you will end up in one of those valleys we discussed in chapter 8, and it is not a place you will enjoy spending your time.

Carry your goals on an index card in your pocket or purse, put the list up on your mirror in your bathroom, on your sun visor of your car, on your desk, and when you accomplish a goal treat yourself. Celebrate, and set a new goal to replace the one you have reached.

When you attain one of your goals, whatever it is, celebrate & reward yourself for your accomplishment. **Be happy, proud of yourself, after all this is about as good as it gets, so pat yourself on the back.**

When you have a list of six or seven goals written down and you have accomplished two or three of them, revise the list, and add a couple of new goals to the list. One of the sayings I have heard: 'out of sight, out of mind.' Even if this list of goals is in several of the locations I have mentioned to put them in this chapter realize sometimes they can be right in front of you, and you won't see them for a few days. When you think of eating because you are hungry, think of your goals, when you get up of the morning think of your goals, it gives you something to get out of bed for! When you are having a bad day, two or three things go wrong, you don't get a listing you expected, or a sale falls out of escrow, think of your goals!

If you do not already have goals in writing with dates, why not take six minutes and write them down before going on to the next chapter? If you say you don't have time, you don't have time <u>not</u> to. While waiting on a client, resting from a workout, taking a break from mowing the lawn, waiting in line at the post office, take that time to write down your goals, **you are a great person, there is no one on the face of the earth like you, you owe it to yourself, to do this NOW! Remember... goals help you to focus!**

Don't be afraid to go out on a limb, that's where the fruit is.

Unknown

Chapter Thirteen

Follow Up Is To Business Growth
What Breathing Is To Life

Myth: If the person is not buying or selling in the next four days to four weeks you are wasting your time with them.

Reality: If a person is interested in selling or buying a home it may be three months or even two years in the future. This is 'potential' business!

This chapter may prove to be the most beneficial of the entire book in order to help you see a twenty, fifty, or even a one hundred percent increase in your business! When I implemented this during the first nine months the increase in growth was an 80% increase for my real estate business. And I had been in the business for over twenty-three years at the time! Thanks to World Class Coaches.

If you have been in the business some time and are not happy, this might be the turning point for you!

For most of my 25 years in real estate sales I was taught, or at least I interpreted the training to say, if the prospect is not interested in buying or selling in the next thirty days, they are suspect. Forget about them and find someone else! **THAT IS NOT TRUE! PLEASE, PLEASE, PLEASE read this chapter carefully.**

There is a good chance if you picked up this book and want to improve an existing real estate sales business, or are considering getting into the real estate business and are serious enough to read this book, and you are excited about what you have read thus far, there is a good chance you can or will become quite successful in selling real estate.

Now to generate even more excitement, let me give you one very simple example. As we will discuss in chapter 18 The Hidden Gold Mine: In October and November 2003, three of the closings I had, were listing leads I generated in May of 2003. By taking the information of the person who told me they planned to sell three or six months down the road following up with them every few weeks to keep in touch, my persistence turned into more than $14,000 income more than five months later! Not only that, some of those clients used me again or referred others to me in later months!

You might want to stop now, and go back, and read the previous paragraph again. It just may help you generate a huge increase in income an additional six months, or even eighteen months from now.

Think about it from a different perspective. Can you recall times in the past when someone talked to you about their services whether it was a roofer, painter, insurance agent, or stock broker, and you said: "no, not now, maybe later." They called you again; and hung in there a few months then when you were in more of a position to do something, you were happy they cared enough to remind you of their availability (services).

Now let's think of the roofer, painter, hair stylist, or handyman, who asked for business and you said you were not interested and never heard from them again. Well perhaps thirty days or three months later, when you really needed their services, and you didn't know how to contact them, or you had forgotten about them. With this second category of people it is much more difficult to recall their situation whereas the first example, perhaps not only did you use their services... you did it over and over again, referred other business to them and perhaps they even became a close friend.

Want something to make you think even more seriously on this matter?

For about fifteen years I used the same loan officer, and then along came a loan officer named Tom Ames. My clients (Larry & Janet Queen) wanted me to use Tom for their real estate transaction, as well as their son's and the next thing you know I used this loan officer again and again. Now almost three years later I continue to refer clients to Tom because of his accountability, dependability, follow up, and reliability, I am tied with one other Realtor in providing this person more mortgage business than all the other Realtors they work with.

So you understand both sides of this story, the loan officer who I used for nearly fifteen years, started slipping, not calling me, not following up consistently, not checking in with me, not doing follow up to people to pre qualify them as quickly as I preferred.

This is sort of the same way some marriages end. The husband and wife quit communicating with each other regularly.

This is one of the easiest items to implement into your business, however CAUTION. It can also be one that is easiest to slip away from doing properly on a continuing basis.

Take some time and study these two words: pushy and persistent. You will learn they are as close as to having the same meaning, but are actually very far apart. Can we suggest? The sun is shining somewhere, there is not a cloud in the sky, the sky is blue, and it is so hot you are perspiring? But, somewhere else, the sun is shining, there is not a cloud in the sky, the sky is blue, and the temperature is minus 20 degrees. Point being… there is a fine line between pushy and persistent.

When anyone tells you that you are pushy there is a good chance it is over, finished, taps, lights out, and the end for that potential business opportunity. And, **when a person thanks you for being persistent, they are paying you a compliment!** When you are able to reach this fine line and be persistent and do it consistently with everyone, you are on your way to more sales, more fun, more happiness, and really enjoying life!

Ladies and Gentlemen: **if you do your "FOLLOW UP" on a regular basis calling that person every two to three weeks, your business will grow,** yet you will have time for family, golf, spirituality, racket ball, weekends off, and time to spend in nature and enjoying your life! Take every Sunday off! Set a goal right now to not work more than three to twelve Sundays during the next twelve months. If you are doing fifty transactions per year you should never have to present more than one or two offers on a Sunday afternoon.

Since we are on follow up, let me mention one item to closely follow up on, and that is returning calls. *Do it and do it promptly.* Even though there are millions of people making more money than you who do not carry a cell phone with them.

It is reasonable for you to not be available for two hours every morning while doing your lead generation, while you are on a listing appointment, Sunday mornings or while in church, on the golf course, or at the beach with your family. Your clients will appreciate that you have a life. They know you will call them back when you are available.

Those who can see the invisible
Can do the impossible.

Unknown

Chapter Fourteen

A TIME TO LAUGH, and A TIME TO CRY, A TIME TO PLAY, and A TIME TO WORK

Myth: This is a serious business; there is no time for play.

Reality: As you move forward working & counseling with people, you need a sense of humor you will soon see you can have fun with people, as well as enjoy this business.

Consider some of what you read in this book you will not agree with, and would never consider doing. And that is ok. Also consider ideas from other sources you may not agree with. And, if you can just get two or three ideas that work really well for you, then you have ideas that can change your life and business drastically.

Take control of your life. If you don't other people will. Schedule and plan time for laughter and there will be some that comes when you least expect it, while you are working or while you are crying things will happen to generate laughter.

Just to make sure you reap all the benefits available in life. SCHEDULE your year, month, week, as well as the day. Take a weekend before Monday comes and have that week completely planned out: there will always be unexpected positive and negative events that come into play which will require adjustments. For the most part though, you will still be making the decisions.

Let me give you an example: I have more than six people with whom I enjoy playing golf and Thursday is my golf afternoon or as of late Tuesday & Friday mornings Once every two or three months it may be changed to Wednesday however in most cases if there is a listing appointment to be set, it is up to me to decide when. Your doctor's office will give you some options however you will come to see the doctor on the options they offer you. On Tuesday morning you talk with someone who wants you to list their home and you offer Wednesday afternoon at 1:15 p.m. or 4:30 p.m. If that does not work for them, offer another time such as Friday at 6:00 p.m. or even Thursday evening at 6:45 p.m., and don't be ashamed of it! That is your time; you stop every few hundred miles and fill your gasoline tank or every 3,000 miles for an oil change in order to take care of your automobile. *Take care of yourself as well.* Schedule that time off, to be with the family, then the other openings in the week can be for your lead generating, listing appointments, and buyer appointments.

Based on what I read in a golf magazine for men, 97 is the average golf score, and I have became better than average. One of the ways I have accomplished this is to leave the pager and the cell phone in the car when I take my golf clubs out. Those next four to five hours are mine to enjoy with my friends and excel my golf game! This is a time for play!

I hope you don't take your cell phone to church with you, if so turn it off, better yet leave it in the car. If there is an emergency someone will call 911 for you. I have heard cell phones ring in church and it is embarrassing to me even though it is not my phone ringing. That is not only embarrassing, it is rude, inconsiderate, ill-mannered and disgraceful! Enough said.

In January 2000 my mother passed away at the age of 90, a wonderful person, a great mother, when she was 87 years old, I would still ask her if she would like me to teach her how to drive. She would always laugh and say: "Now you know I can't drive" and my response were always: "we don't know until you try; and if you can't I will teach you." And she'd laugh.

During that time of the loss of my mother, I grieved., I thought of so many things she had taught me, of the simple life I had as a child growing up, she and my dad did all they could for me. I had some deep thoughts and memories during that time, and I took off from work for that time.

I invited my broker, and close Realtor friends to the memorial service, it was a great time. We celebrated her life, and her moving onward to be with God. Then I moved on with my life and business.

You decide on the time to work. Will it be three hours a day, ten hours a day and will it be three days a week or six days a week. Most importantly schedule that play time and laughter time in that week. Don't let work interrupt the play time; and as well, don't be playing when you have work scheduled.

The following is one example that can help you make major changes in your life, have people feel better about you, give you more control, and still communicate promptly.

Change the recording on your cell phone to: "This is____ you have reached my cell phone, I do not answer the phone while driving or when I am with a client. Leave a message and I will call you as soon as I am available." This makes an impression! It makes a statement! It lets people know that if they are a client they are important especially if they are with you, and it lets people realize you are a safe driver. Now if some of the time you decide to answer the phone while you are driving or if you are with a buyer, is up to you. On listing appointments I recommend *always leaving the cell phone in the car!*

The Journey of a thousand miles starts with a Single step.

Ancient Chinese proverb

Chapter Fifteen

Every Transaction is Different

If you are considering getting a real estate license, or just got one recently you may have an expectation of what happens in this business, however should you choose to stay in the business, you eventually realize, (even though you think this transaction will be like one in the past,) that no two transactions are the same in what happens during the process all the way to the final recordation of the deed and you receiving your commission check from your broker.

Because of this, I feel it is one aspect of the business that makes it not only unique but also interesting and exciting as opposed to boring. There is that ongoing curiosity as to what the next transaction will be like, what the seller will be like, the buyer, the co-broking Realtor; what are the backgrounds and of each of these peoples personalities, motivation, goals, needs and desires.

What you need to understand from the beginning is this; just because the close of escrow date is written in the purchase contract, does not mean it will close on or before that date. Although almost all of my transactions have closed on the date called for in the purchase agreement you may from time, to time have extenuating circumstances.

It is common nature when this happens, for you to determine if someone is trying to hide something by attempting to gracefully pull out of the transaction. In most cases this is not the situation. It is not your job to an attorney, a police officer or a private investigator; however it is your responsibility to honor your fiduciary duties of loyalty, obedience, disclosure, and confidentiality to your client!

It is very important in representing your client, if there is a reason to extend the close of escrow date, or time is needed on extending any inspection periods, to communicate with the other Realtor and get the extension signed by all parties in a timely fashion. No one likes that *extension* word, however it is better to disclose the issues not being met in the agreement, and get an extension signed prior to or past the last day, in order to keep everyone in the loop as we say.

The situation can become stressful if plans have to be changed, therefore if you represent the buyer and you see something is going to hold things up, let the other Realtor know. Communicate in advance and in writing with the seller to get an extension signed, so they can convey the information to the party whose home they are moving into, in order to have as smooth a transaction as possible.

On your 25th or 100th or 424th closing you will have things happen that you have never had happen before! Some examples: (1) one of the buyers or sellers passes away after the contracts have been accepted, but before close of escrow. (2) The buyers or sellers decide they no longer want to live in unity, and want a divorce. (3) The seller or buyer decided to go on vacation without telling anyone, and do not have a telephone number where they can be reached. (4) The buyers' loan is denied just two days before closing when the lender calls to verify one of the buyer's income and the verification reveals the buyer will no longer be employed with the company in thirty days. (5) There is a severe storm, which does substantial damage to the home, and even though the insurance company makes the repairs the buyer no longer wants to own the property. (6) Due to issues over the home inspection, buyer decides to not purchase the home. (7) Seller decides not to sell. 8. Buyer decides they do not want this home. These are just a very few. Go ask your broker to give you two or three more and then ask a couple of other agents in your office to give you some situations they have experienced.

I have been extremely fortunate throughout several hundred transactions, to have very few not make it once they were started and all signatures were on the agreement. Also very fortunate, to have never had a law suit or complaint filed against me; however, at least one of these could happen on the next transaction. This is why you must always be very cautious about everything you say and do with everyone involved in every transaction.

You don't ever want to be in the position where the transactions closes, and because of your actions, either because of what you have done, not done, said or not said, your client is in the position to never consider recommending you to anyone in the future who is thinking of buying or selling real estate.

I am not judged by the number of times I fail, but by the number of times I succeed; and the number of times I succeed are in direct proportion to the number of times I can fail, but keep trying.

Tom Hopkins

Chapter Sixteen

ECSTATIC-EXCITEMENT-MOTIVATION
If you have this you will succeed

Take time to review chapter eight again and make a commitment to yourself now, (not next month, next week, or tomorrow) that if you associate with comes to mind when you read that chapter, you will consciously find reasons to move and avoid them! I know this is a strong statement; however I did say politely, to "find reasons to move on." Let me help you; think of people you went to school with, worked with in former employment positions, neighbors, a distant aunt or uncle, whom you have not seen in a year or so. You moved on for one reason because you had enough in common with each other to stay in touch.

You can manage with this change just as you did with changes in the past. Change is difficult. To help you with this, **the top three most stressful situations are: death of a loved one, divorce, and being fired from ones job.** If you can look at it you <u>can</u> pull away (disassociate yourself) from the associate who reminds you of bees, snakes or broken glass.

Now let's change our state of mind and get on with this chapter. Read this paragraph and then sit back in a comfortable place where no one is around, close your eyes and think for a couple minutes.

Here we go; I want you to think of a time...

When you were on top of the world, do you remember how you felt? You will read in chapter 22 of the Pumpkin Man in his orange suit and green shoes flying around in helicopters and landing on hospital roofs in order to see the children and give them free pumpkins & candy? You will see he rode in a gold Rolls Royce convertible in an orange suite and threw out 500 pounds of candy along the pumpkin parade route. When you are in this mindset, **you are unstoppable;** you can pick up that telephone and prospect for an hour or two and always get a lead or two or even set an appointment or two. You can go take the listing you are going on, you will sell the buyer a home today of the three homes you are showing them, you will …… you will …. You can …. **You can do anything when you are on this level.**

Now think about this, have you ever considered what life would be like if you could experience ten or twenty days a month on this level? What would life be like, how much would your business grow if you could spend one hour a day on a high like this?

Is this not realistic? Ok let's look at the worse case scenario. Let's just say it is possible but not realistic, now, I would like you to put this book down now, get a piece of paper and write some of your own personal times in the past where you experienced ecstasy, as I have shared some of mine above with you, and in detail in chapter 22.

Did you stop and write them down? Couldn't think of any? Then put the book down until you do! I will give you another one. My mother and dad making snow cream when I was five years old. That may have been the best tasting food I ever put in my mouth! It doesn't matter how far back in the past it was; put the book down and write a list for yourself!

Think about this. When you experience a down time, a time in your real estate business where it is not the best, or may even be the worst time you have ever experienced. You are having some serious financial problems, issues with your spouse, or with your children if you need to talk to someone but you are embarrassed to do so now is the time to look at that memory list you wrote down. If you still haven't done it, do it now! Please… **Put this book down and make that list we have been talking about!**

Now make a strong commitment, the strongest commitment you have ever made to yourself in your life to take just five minutes every day for the next twenty-one days to read, study, & look at what you have written down. It is ok to make a copy or two of it and have a copy lying in the bathroom and possibly a copy in your car so on the way to a listing appointment you can review what you have written down! Close your eyes *(except when driving)* each time you do this, and visualize where you want to be so when you are finished, you feel as though you have actually been in that place, in that time again. Make it so focused and intense that when you wake up you really have to shake your head to get yourself to realize, it was a dream; you are here in this moment?

This is the power I want you to experience! Give yourself just five minutes a day for the next twenty one days to review your list of the most ecstatic times in your life. Oh what the heck, while you are doing this, it sounds so exciting, let's just add a couple items, just to help you keep your mind occupied.

Make a list of goals if *anything were possible of* what you would like to accomplish in the next week, thirty days, or ninety days. And read these goals often. What would really be great is if you were to call me or email me and let me know what happened during those 21 or 90 days.

Risk more than others think is safe.
Care more than others think is wise.
Dream more than others think is practical.
Expect more than others think is possible.
                                     Claude T. Bissell

Dan McGinnis...Outstanding in his field.

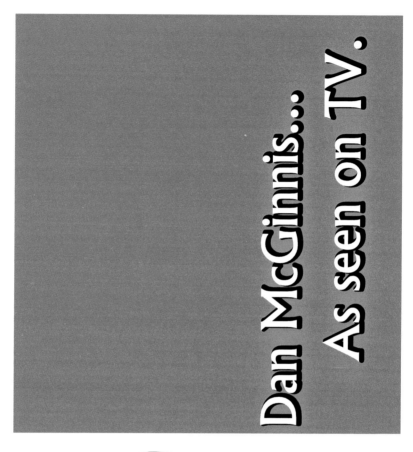

Dan McGinnis...
As seen on TV.

Want to sell your home? Call Dan, he will *DRIVE* buyers to it.

List your home with Dan.... He will get right on it.

For your real estate needs...
Call Dan he will go to bat for you.

Dan McGinnis...
In a class all by himself.

WITHOUT Dan McGinnis as *Your* Realtor

WITH Dan McGinnis as *Your* Realtor

PART III

PERSONAL MARKETING & PROMOTION

Some might call this part the meat and potatoes, others may say the icing on the cake. To me, it is a very exciting area. You will learn how to host the greatest party you have ever attended. All about geographical farming, this is a <u>must read </u>area which I have enjoyed immensely. After all, if it is really fun and you enjoy it, if you are helping people and making money at the same time; how much better can it get?

We will discuss things that are **NOT A DUPLICATES of the AVERAGE idea.** They are unique. The Hidden Gold Mine chapter has to be a favorite of mine because just in the past six months this is what increased my income by 90% and not one copper Lincoln was spent doing it! Oh I suppose I did spend about $25.00 for thank you cards, envelopes and postage stamps. Recognize the techniques for advertising and making a profit, instead of having an ego issue, and learn to have pride in yourself and what you do. Following are examples of very successful postcard campaigns I initiated. Hope they inspire greatness!

Chapter Seventeen

Geographical Farming

Myth: Geographical farming is not a way to make money.

Reality: This area can grow over months and years and can be your livelihood in the future!

First let me say if you are in a hurry, looking for a quick fix, or a rapid increase in real estate sales income, this is not the area you will find it! However, this could be the best foundation you could ever have in residential real estate sales.

This is an area that could really make the difference in succeeding and not succeeding in real estate for you in months and years to come. The reason I say this is because it is one of the areas I started out with in Columbus, Ohio, and have done in three different areas in Phoenix, Arizona. And it was fun!

Just some suggestions, do some research. Take a few days to come to a decision on a farm area, if one of your goals is to do farming. Look to see if it is an area that is appreciating as well, or better, than other areas within your reach for marketing. Look at the history of the area, the turnover, if it is an area for retirees they may all be settled in and not moving as much as other areas.

It doesn't have to be a geographical farm. You could farm, non owner occupant homes, you could farm the obituaries, this may sound a bit morbid but someone will get business from this area, after all we all will die sooner or later that's for sure, and not a bad word if you have lived right, you may be going to a better home!

For our purposes, we will focus strictly on geographical farming. Just as an example, I have had as many as five signs with my name on them in the front yards of a 550-home farm, along with two or three other real estate signs, from different agents and different real estate companies. You are in control when you have that! You've arrived! Those statements sound really powerful don't they?

Do not expect any business what-so-ever during the first six months you begin a farm area. I believe you will have business, and when you do not expect it, when it comes you will feel much better about yourself and the area of business you have chosen to specialize in. Don't overwork yourself. Take an hour or two, every three or four days a week to work on knocking on doors, telephone calling, or delivering some marketing item door to door. Remember, there are other areas of marketing we have discussed in this book you should consider devoting some time to as well. If appropriate for the area do a mailing a minimum of every thirty days.

Farming is something that can really be fun. You are getting out and meeting people, and over time seeing them again and again, you get to know them, they get to know you. And they can become as influential as a past client when it comes to referrals.

Let me give you an example in addition to The World's Largest Residential Pumpkin Parade (chapter 22 for my farm area.) Creating and organizing a neighborhood yard sale is something I did when I was farming an area we lived in. Over a period of about two years we had yard sales in October and April (twice a year). It grew to over a 150-family neighborhood yard sale. It served a couple of purposes for my area. Some people began to put stuff out in their front yard every few weeks and it did not look appealing to me, so I decided to help them sell their stuff, by generating more customers so they could make more money in a shorter period of time and then put the stuff not sold, away for another six months. It worked well. I ran ads in local newspapers to come to our home for a free map of the 150-family neighborhood yard sale.

Let me fine tune this for you. You see there were approximately 70 to 110 homes participating and several of those had their friends or relatives who lived in other areas of town bring their "stuff" to set up and sell in their front yard.

It was like the county fair, people were selling food and kids were selling Kool-aid. To give you some idea of what was going on here the street where they came to get their map and other information with my name on it was bumper to bumper traffic parked on BOTH sides of the street for four blocks. You couldn't find a place to park on that street for almost four hours! They would park, get a map, walk to a couple of yard sales, and see a couple more, the next thing they knew they were on another street. Some people even forgot where they parked their car!

Well guess what happened? When several hundred people came to our front yard for a free map of participating yard sales, they all got something with my name on it, my telephone number, the name of the real estate company I worked with, and usually something they could keep, such as a scratch pad, helium filled balloons, (of course with my company name, my name and telephone number on them.) We also made up Peanut Farm Kits with my name, (which they would keep for months, because of the directions on how to grow your own peanuts; great learning experience for the kids! We even had school teachers request that I bring peanut farm kits to their classroom for each of their students, or a Pumpkin Man Mighty Grip.

You have the same opportunity available to you Just put YOUR NAME ON THEM!

From time to time I would ask if they had any interest in buying or selling a home. I don't believe there was ever a yes answer from anyone. However, when someone in the neighborhood thought of selling you know who they thought of first for a Realtor? Not just the people whom I helped sell their stuff, but also the people who had no interest in selling and didn't like others having yard sales every other weekend, because they saw it helped keep the streets clean.

Going through the neighborhood knocking on doors, always smile when you meet someone at the door. Always have something to leave with them, with your name and telephone number on it, something they can use. Follow up with 'thank you notes' to those you talk with. This can be your real estate income if you work it right!

You might want to start with a couple of hundred homes, and depending on how you feel about this type of marketing, in a year or so choose another area as well, or add a few hundred homes to the initial farm area.

It was quite amusing during my time of farming, to see another Realtor or two, once in a while hang something on our door, unfortunately for them, they never came back a second time, as it takes multiple repeat returns to build a successful farm area. Unfortunately they didn't know that. What was really funny was when a neighbor would call me and tell on some Realtor! That's right! I had a few people who would call me when they had a real estate agent knock on their door (in my farm area) or leave something on their door and let me know someone was working "in my area." It was really hilarious when my wife answered the telephone and got the message from the neighbor before I got home later in the day.

Remember, as in all other areas of sales, to be asking a lot of questions instead of telling people things. In an area for instance of 300 homes, you have 300 potentials there. Each of those three hundred each have parents or grandparents, mother and father-in-laws, other relatives and friends. That 300 who know you, can turn into 1,800, over a period of six to eighteen months, so when you go into five or six years, you really have strength built up in that community!

I know some of you high tech agents are wondering why emails, faxes etc have not been discussed here. Read my next book to be published in early of 2005. **THE FORGOTTEN ART...** I am not saying do not use email, I just KNOW FOR A FACT this STILL WORKS.

Do your mailings in order for them to be received on Thursday, Friday or Saturday. There is less junk mail and bills on those days coming in the mail, be sure and check with your local mail carriers on this.

What hath God wrought
Samuel F. B. Morse

Chapter Eighteen

The Hidden Gold Mine

This chapter may be all you need to read to have your business take off like a rocket! With a very strong foundation, and if you focus and follow these steps you can…

KEY POINT that "hidden gold mine." and in most instances it is ever so slightly hidden. **It DOES require patience,** and if I can do it, **I know you can!** Because I may be in the top percentage of people with the least patience.

One of the advantages to this area of residential real estate is, no one else is doing it. Partly because of the talk about of 'the do not call' list. And even if they did do it, the average licensee would quit just before it is about to turn into a growing business.

Another advantage of the hidden gold mine area is that it only takes thirty to ninety minutes a day. In order to accomplish this timeframe and attain the highest possible results, there are a few initial issues we must accomplish.

CONSIDER THIS: If you are a baseball fan let's look at Randy Johnson, pitcher for the Arizona Diamondbacks. When he is on the mound pitching he is not thinking about his wife and children, how he loves them, what they will do tomorrow, and next week or even after the game is over! He is not thinking about the bad game he had the day before. He does not have his cell phone with him. His entire focus is on that pitch! Stick with me, I am going somewhere with this, no matter how elementary it sounds. I want you to get everything you need to be a great success if you choose this as one of the areas you work in real estate.

CONSIDER THIS: When Tiger Woods is putting on the 8th green he is not thinking about what happened on the 6th or 7th hole. He is not thinking about the drive he hit on the 8th hole, nor is he even thinking about his second shot or approach shot to the 8th green. His mind is only on <u>sinking that putt!</u>

CONSIDER THIS: When you are praying your mind is focused on thanking God for your blessings or asking for help in some way. If your thoughts jump off on to something else you immediately bring your focus back to where it should be. And I would think, when you are praying you don't usually have your cell phone and pager with you.

You see… if you follow this process it will work and work great! If you don't it won't! It's that simple. That was simple wasn't it?

Let's set the stage… you have your telephone numbers whether 500 or 5,000. It does not matter. You will want to have a headset, another tool that is necessary. Estimated cost… less than $100. It helps the nerves and muscles in the neck, hands arms, and frees you up to take notes while the person is talking, so you recall what they have said, and have accurate information. You will want a clean area and desk from which to work.

Now to some VERY IMPORTANT ISSUES. If there are any other telephones in your area, turn them off or unplug them! If you have a cell phone with you take it to the trunk of your car, or turn it off, and do not turn it back on until your lead generation time is completed! If you have a pager, bury it in the desk drawer or somewhere you will not look for it if it goes off. For the next thirty minutes to two hours this is critical.

Let's go a little deeper into this. If you receive a call that there is a problem with an escrow, someone is calling to cancel their listing appointment with you, one of your family members has a personal problem they want help with, a friend is lonesome and just want to talk with you, your lender called just to let you know interest rates were going up, your lender called to let you know interest rates were going down, another Realtor called to say they could not get the lockbox to open on one of your listings, your doctor called with your blood test results, the baby sitter called to say the dog ran away, someone called to say a relative passed away, someone called to say a relative had been admitted to the hospital, Believe me folks…Any of these can wait an hour without your help or attention.

Do you carry a cell phone to church or a baseball or basketball game? Well I hope you do not and if you do it is turned off. The cell phone has become a *bad habit*; *we think* we <u>have</u> to answer it. I call people and say "I hope I caught you at a half way decent time" and they answer "no I was eating, or no I was on my way out to the airport" you begin to wonder, well why did you answer the telephone?! We all do that from time to time, however if we work to rid ourselves of that habit our lives will be more organized on the issue at hand.

This is ideal for the new licensee in the market place to build your business when you have no business as well as for the agent who wants to increase their existing business. The only cost is one to two hours a day of your time initially. I recommend you take advantage of all the other areas such as everyone you know. When I first became licensed while I was going to school in Columbus Ohio, I told everyone I saw I was going to be a Realtor. My first three transactions were with others who I worked with side by side in a bicycle accessory warehouse, and the a sergeant I knew in the U.S. Army Reserves.

In addition to that I did geographical farming, which worked well also, now that I think back, there was another Realtor farming the same subdivision. She was experienced, and got business there from her farming. One thing we had in common, I GOT BUSINESS ALSO from the same subdivision.

If you are seriously considering this business or are already a Realtor and want to go to a higher level of number of transactions and income, this may be the best possible chapter for you to read!

First choose two or three areas you would like to search for sellers in. It can be geographical however there are other ways as well, such as anyone whose name begins with 'Mc' which I have done that and I was astonished by the response. If you speak Spanish, you might want to choose Hispanic names because you have an immediate rapport and something in common with Spanish speaking people.

Some examples: choose an area of homes in the $400,000 to $700,000 price range as well as homes from $100,000 to $300,000 price range. Other examples would be some homes within one or two miles north and east of your office location, and going four to seven miles to the south and west of your office location.

Find a source for obtaining the telephone numbers of the homeowners in your chosen selections. Depending on your local association or your broker, you may need to sift the telephone numbers through the National Do Not Call List. Or, if it is appropriate, some title companies provide telephone numbers through a company that does the scrubbing through the 'do not call list.'

Variety is created here. Let me explain. You don't eat tossed salad every day, or drink the same drink every day, day after day. You don't eat pizza every day seven days a week. Or at least I hope you don't. We as Americans are extremely fortunate to have a variety in our lives from which to choose from.

When playing golf you don't use the same club for each shot, neither is each hole the same distance.

This might be a good time to go back and read from the beginning of this chapter again. Why? Because it is so simple, possibly too simple to make sense. **Understand... this is coming from someone who has done this, who has tried about every marketing idea in over 25 years as a Realtor in Ohio and Arizona, someone who is not the best salesman, doesn't make the most money, who is not the greatest Realtor that ever lived, (but who currently as of this writing, IS DOING IT, NOW) & has a strong desire to be honest, fair, kind, loving and provide the very best service to each client!**

In many instances, your potential clients may have bought two to three years ago or longer, and were not satisfied with their Realtor, or perhaps their Realtor never stayed in touch with them after the transaction closed. Even if they remembered the Realtor they are not married to that person. So if you happen to come along at the right time, and are polite, professional, and persistent you just might stand a good chance of getting their business!

Now let's look at those hundreds of people who have no connection with a Realtor. I know because I talk to them five or six days a week every week! And I only talk to ten new people every day! Oh ok, I will admit I sometimes am feeling so good I go an extra two to five contacts in any given day. This is one of the most successful areas I have worked in my 25 year career of real estate sales. Remember... you must fine tune what you ask, when you call, and how you say it!

GET READY, GET SET, HERE IS THE EXAMPLE:

 The pauses are very critical as well.
"Hi, Jane, this is _____; PAUSE; I hope I caught you at a half way decent time?" PAUSE I am a Realtor with _____, and I was calling PAUSE to see PAUSE if you folks PAUSE had possibly thought of PAUSE selling your home?" "No", "Thank you for your time." Many times they will say 'yes' that you have caught them at a half way decent time. If they say "No I was on my way out the door,"

say: "Ok this will just take a second. I was calling to see PAUSE if you folks PAUSE had possibly thought of selling your home?"

If the person says "NO," the total time of the call should not have been more than 23 seconds. And you never ask a second question if you get a 'no' to the first question. If they say maybe, proceed with questions that begin with: when, why, where, what, and how. **If they have plans to move within two years, this is a lead!** If less than six months place them in you're "A" category of leads, if it is six months to two years place them in your "B" category.

Write a very short thank you note for their time on the telephone, and mail it the same day. To be sure this is done, when you hang up the telephone, begin to address the envelope! Now place this lead in your computer or on a lead generation form where you will maintain a record of what they have said, when you called them, what and when you mailed them anything. Once it is recorded, go back to the phone for your next lead generation call.

Everyone in the "A" category should receive something in the mail from you every two weeks. Everyone in the "B" category should receive something in the mail from you every four weeks.

Choose a number under ten per day to call. You decide whether it is five or six days a week. With the discipline and patience you will see awesome results!

What to mail? Purchase a newsletter, find real estate articles people might be interested in, or two or three times per month write something yourself i.e. definitions of real estate terms or words, such as: 48-hour first right of refusal. You can write a page on that with examples of how it could benefit a client whether they are the buyer and/or seller! Work along these lines and fine tune your tonality and the pauses where they are indicated.

I am really excited, next week I start mailing a newsletter which I have heard Realtors around the country have received as many as 20 or more leads per month from it. This may be as great as a pumpkin parade. Interested? Call me. This starts September 2004.

There is a difference between this and the person who is trying to shove a timeshare down your throat during a good TV program or evening dinner, which also means you, can do this during the morning starting at 9:00 a.m. ... YES... there are people at home during that time and not at work. You see I know what you are thinking. Remember I am one of you, and I have been for 25 years, I have made telephone calls and talked to more than 40,000 people in the past seven years. Yes, I used to call and speak to between 6,000 and 8,000 people every year. No more... I cut the numbers by two thirds and increased my income by two thirds, thanks to WORLD CLASS COACHES.

In the past (prior to 2003) I even wore two head sets and called two people at the same time, and I have had two answers at the same time and I know how to talk to both of them at the same time! This year I am on target for talking to 2,500 people, (considerably less people than in the past,) but with a much **closer follow up** and a 90% increase in income, thanks to World Class Coaches. STOP! Read the last sentence again, so you don't miss anything.

Some important items to recognize:

From this process, the follow-up process becomes strong and very powerful. As an example last year I closed three transactions in October and November for, around $14,000 in gross commissions from people I initially talked with in May. With those three people there were three or four telephone calls made to them when they were not home or did not choose to answer the telephone, there were six to ten calls where I actually talked with them on the telephone. At the time I was not doing the mailings as aggressively as I just explained to you, so they got about five to seven mailings, during that six month time frame. Be sure you keep you're A's @ one mailing every two weeks, precisely!

As mentioned in chapter 13, follow-up is very important to lead generation.

Let's look at the breakdown associated with this process:
- **No advertising in print**
- **No internet advertising**
- **No open houses**

From a total of approximately-21 telephone conversations of 45 seconds to ten minutes long with three different people, and just over one and a half hours on the telephone and $7.80 in postage. I grossed over $14,000. So if my time is worth $100/ hour, I spent just under $125.00 for a $14,000 return, and this does not include any referral business that has since come from these three clients!

God has blessed me with courage, discipline, determination, motivation, desire, patience, faith, habits, expectation and consistency. I know that many people say they cannot do this, they can't pick up the telephone, and they can't call people.

If you are one of those, let me see if I can analyze it a bit more. You pick up the receiver, listen to the dial tone or put on your head set, have a seven or ten digit number to call. You press the buttons, it rings three to four times, and you hang up, repeat the process someone answers the telephone, their voice scares you, what do you do next? HANG UP THE TELEPHONE!

Now pick up the telephone again, using the same process. Someone answers. Have your words written out and read: first their name: Hi, Richard? This is____, I hope I caught you at a half way decent time… (refer back a couple of pages to the complete process.) SAY THIS SLOW!

Now, I will give you some of the worst case scenarios I have ever had in talking with 40,000 different people. This is the worse thing they will ever say to you:

1. They hang up the telephone while you are talking. WHY? They are in a bad mood, they are mad at their mother, they are mad at their son, they are mad at themselves, or at their spouse the dog just ruined the living room carpet, or they were once in sales and failed at it and are jealous of you. They are in foreclosure and depressed, or their car was just repossessed.

2. They cuss at you and hang up. (I am guessing 10 out of 40,000)

3. They cuss at you and try to annoy you and when they see they can't they hang up. (Let's say maybe 15 out of 40,000)

4. They say "no thank you," before you ask the question and hang up. (Approximately 27 out of 40,000)

5. They say "I am on the other line can you call me back?" You don't call them back because 100 times out of 100 either they won't answer the telephone, or you will get the answering machine!

6. They tell you they are a Realtor. And you ask "well why you are not out working?" (Just kidding)

7. They tell you they are going to real estate school right now.

8. They have a relative who is a Realtor.
9. Their home is currently listed with a Realtor. Oh, on this one be sure it is listed and confirm it doesn't happen to be a FSBO, because if it is a FSBO. **This is a lead!**

10 They say they are not interested; however they say "THANK YOU" before hanging up on you.

The ten examples listed above are two fold, it is my way of being funny, it is also for those of you who are actually fearful of the telephone and it is my sincere way of letting you see the truth.

Ok, there is one other item I did not tell you, just so you know and don't think you are weird or think your telephone is not working or something. You will dial anywhere from one to forty telephone numbers sometimes before someone answers the telephone, or you may talk to your "five contacts" in the first ten or fifteen attempts.

In summarizing I suggest that you strongly consider rereading this chapter a couple of times, getting your list of telephone numbers ready, and spending just one hour a day, five to six days a week on this area for a week, then a month, then two months. If by that time you have not seen unbelievable results, consider stopping the process. Or Take a break. **Or getting professional coaching to improve your success, call me and I will put you in touch with a company who can possibly help YOU!**

When the desire to achieve something
Is stronger than the negative effects
Of your Daily activities... you'll succeed.

Unknown

Chapter Nineteen

A Clever Idea

A couple of years ago, my wife and I moved into our new home. I had had an idea for a couple of years in the back of my mind, however to me; the floor plan of our home of 18 years was just not conducive to the idea.

The new home is ideal for the idea, and we have implemented it about seven times, in the first twenty four months. Each time it gets better. Sort of like a pumpkin parade starting in front of your home, but different. Not near as much work, planning, and money is necessary.

You may be different than me, but most of my closest friends are either past clients or people who have referred buyers or sellers to me. To be able to get together and laugh, and have a great time with friends, is a great pleasure for me.

Are you ready? Here we go. I invited about thirty five people to our home for a: CLIENT APPRECIATION DINNER PARTY. The first time, we purchased meat balls from an Italian restaurant, and gourmet deserts; everything else my wonderful wife prepared.

She had such an enjoyable time, and had so many compliments that she has prepared the rest of the dinner parties. That's right everything! (If you are hungry right now you better not read the rest of this) Turkey breast, meatballs, ham, yams, potatoes, corn, fresh baked bread, apple salad, potato salad, fresh baked coconut cream pie, fresh strawberry pie, and fresh home made cookies. Oh the one next month… I am making **HOME MADE ICE CREAM!**

Each dinner party gets better, always twenty-five to forty people, (no alcoholic beverages) we even added door prizes. Everyone who attends has their name placed in a hat, and after about an hour there are drawings for prizes.

My wife is an awesome shopper. She bought two Norelco triple-head electric razors, for four dollars each. John Behun's name was drawn for one of the Norelco electric razors; I had driven 20 miles one way to bring them to the party as John said it was too far to drive. Since he won a razor he liked so well, he is now ready to bring his wonderful wife, Bertha and drive himself, the next time. Although names are drawn out of a hat, my wife always has more than enough prizes in order for everyone there to get something, even the kids.

At one of the parties, as things were toning down, there were two couples starting to leave, and all of the prizes had not yet been given away, so I quickly said it is time for another drawing. One of my former clients does work for me and others as a handyman, Ryan Ridgeway – he is great. I had a check for him for $1500 for payment of work he had done. I whispered in his ear and told him what I was going to do.

Just as these two couples were about to leave I called out his name really loud and said: "a check for One Thousand Five Hundred Dollars!" It was so funny to watch our friends do a double take, turn around and come back to see just what might be drawn out next.

At our last dinner party, I hired a professional magician! He was great, everyone liked him, there were lots of laughs, he moved about to different groups of people showing his magic. We will have him back for sure the next time!

Since we started the Client Appreciation dinner parties I have found a couple of other Realtors who have done the same thing only they have everyone come to a restaurant which is just not personal enough for me. Besides it is also really neat to be able to mix with many friends and former clients and not have to leave home to do it.

IF THERE IS NO WIND, row.
Latin Proverb

Chapter Twenty

An Extraordinary Idea

We have always heard it is better to give than to receive, also when you give it will come back to you ten fold. It seems to me when we give; we never consider receiving something in return; however it seems to always happen. Sometimes, the next day, sometimes the next month.

Should you decide to do what I discuss in this chapter, I just want you to know I am about to take it upon myself to do again. It has been a little over two and one half years since I did it, and I didn't do everything I could have or even should have.

I just made a few calls, thought of a few ideas, did it and let it drop. Well, I suppose I made more than just a few calls. To me two is a couple and three is a few. So I will admit, I made a couple of hundred calls, but what else do you have to do with your time as a real estate agent after lead generation, presenting any offers you might have, and listing appointments. What do you do?

Maybe we should have an entire chapter on planning one's time, as well as a business plan. More on that in the next book.

We all hear of ideas throughout our career, in many cases I feel few of us pursue any of them, and to be honest some of them are not worth pursuing. I do feel though you will find this to be of significant value, and that is: a referral directory.

Now we are not talking about some real estate agent giving you a buyer or seller referral nor are we talking about you giving another Realtor a referral of a buyer or seller and either of you receiving a referral fee. I am talking about <u>your providing a service to the community.</u>

We often hear horror stories of law suits, complaints filed against real estate agents, and are told to not recommend a home warranty company, title company, or home inspector because if they make a mistake the client may come after you for recommending the company who did them wrong. And I am not disagreeing with that thought, as I have always been very cautious, and too, I feel we still have some rights as American citizens, and if I am totally confident in the company or person providing the service I will continue to recommend them, after all, hundreds of people have recommended me!

Without printing out my first edition of the entire referral directory, I will give you samples, ideas, of everything you need to create your own referral directory.

Once you have it completed, you now have the opportunity to go back to all your past clients, people who gave you names of services to put in the directory as well as all of those who are listed in the directory and personally (face to face) hand each of them a copy. Here again is an opportunity for you to make contact with someone who just might feel obligated to give you the name and telephone number of someone they know who wants to buy or sell a home.

Included in the referral directory or the first page is a message from you. I will give you part of it here to help you along should you decide to create your own referral directory:

Dear Valued Client:
It is my privilege to bring you our Referral Directory (first edition). I would like to take this opportunity to thank those of you who referred us to quality business people for our first edition.
With the aid of my personal assistant, and my wife we have been able to compile this directory. It has taken several months to check on references, compare costs, and gather feedback from our clients who have used the services of those listed.

Although I cannot guarantee the quality of the work any of these people will provide, I feel confident that I can give a strong recommendation for each and every person in this directory. We have included more than one provider of each service wherever possible. PLEASE CALL to tell us who we might add in our second edition.

Sincerely
Dan D. McGinnis, CRS

By the way when you know anyone who may have the need for the services of a Realtor (buying or selling) property I would appreciate your calling me with their name.

And don't forget to print your telephone number a couple of times in your referral directory, as a Realtor.

The second page began with: **PEOPLE ARE TALKING...**
I will give you one of the six comments from past clients I had permission to put in my referral directory.

Thank you for all the help that you gave us on the sale of our home. We had given up on selling the house, because of the past two Realtors but you put it all together for us. You have our permission to use us a reference anytime. Don & Liz Wilkins.

My recommendation to begin this process is to call all of your past clients in your sphere of influence, to include friends and ask them for recommendations of people who they have used. Here are just a few examples: Accountants, Appliance, Appraisers, and Attorneys, Automobile: Mechanic - Paint - Sales. Carpet Cleaning, Carpentry, Glass, Handyman, Locksmith, Electrician, Plumbing, Roofing, Landscaping, Painters, Photo, Printer, Psychotherapist, Restaurants, Title Companies, Miscellaneous.

These represent about half of the referrals used in my first edition. Realize what you are doing here, you are calling people you know and trust, to ask them for people they know and trust, so you can share the list with others who may be in need of a service.

Understand as you collect the list, some of the people you call will be suspicious and wonder what is going on. After all how often does someone do a good deed, asking for no money? Let me give you an example:

"Hi, Robert, my name is Dan McGinnis, I am a Realtor, and one of your customers gave me your name and number and said they were very pleased with the serviced you provided them. I am compiling a referral directory and would like to include your business in it if you would like, in order for me to feel comfortable and confident I need three other references who I may call to see they have been satisfied with your work."

I am not a fisherman;   however I will use this as an example for the referral directory. You could sit on the river bank for maybe two or even three hours, for two or three days with nothing, then catch the largest fish you ever caught in your life.

Your referral directory could work the same way to provide business for you. Just so you have a more complete understanding I will tell you about one situation I experienced.

I did not have a home cleaning service and asked one of the agents in my office who gave me the name of Clear Choice; however when I called the company the person no longer owned it, and the new owner was Mr. James Tripodi. After explaining to him I was creating a referral directory and discussing including him in the directory, he mentioned he and his wife were looking for a home. I offered my services and he let me know he was fine on his own.

We continued the conversation, and he explained he had specific requirements, namely only a home in 85022, or 85028 zip codes and they were in no hurry and only driving around on their own.

I said: "well if you want I could just check, and see what is new a couple times a week and email them to you, save you time and gasoline. He finally agreed with that suggestion, and within a few weeks, I showed them about six homes. We wrote an offer which was accepted and there were two other offers. **KEY POINT:** Neither of the other Realtors were present. They faxed their offers in. At one point one of the sellers raised up out of her chair at the dining room table, looked at me and said: "The other offer is better than your offer" and my response was: "I apologize, I am just doing what the buyer asked, if this won't work for you, please counter the offer."

Mr. & Mrs. Tripodi got the home. **KEY POINT** During the next 20 months they have had me sell another property for them, and referred another buyer, also a seller. They now are good friends, and we play golf together almost four times a month.

I don't like to compare or use numbers, however if it will clarify things for you a bit more, **KEY POINT** *this idea cost less than $1000.* Plus some time in calling, going out and meeting people. The return on the investment within approximately twenty months was really extremely large; four successful closed transactions; two representing buyers and two representing sellers.

Now that you have your copies printed, call everyone you know and offer them a free copy, as well as those who are in the directory, and those who recommended the businesses you put in your directory.

DO NOT GO WHERE THE PATH MAY LEAD; GO INSTEAD WHERE THERE IS NO PATH AND LEAVE A TRAIL. Ralph Waldo Emerson

Chapter Twenty One

ADVERTISING, EGO, PROFIT & PRIDE

The purpose of this chapter is only to get you to think a little, in order to be sure you are on track to make a profit, and that is not a bad word, after all anyone who seeks any type of employment whether by punching a time clock, owning a business, on salary or commission should have one goal in mind; and that is to have money left over for YOU after expenses, taxes, food, and shelter.

Take a close look on a regular basis at your net versus your gross. The reason we discuss this is because of what has developed over the past decade in our industry. And if you are new to the business (the past ten years) it is beneficial for you to see outside of the box.

I am not saying we need to go backwards and do business like we did twenty years ago, because change is good and change is constant. My point is we need to focus on our profit and in doing so we have to pay close attention to our advertising expenses and our ego.

During the late 1970's and most of the 1980's the real estate business (meaning real estate agents) didn't have ego issues (to my knowledge.) We did advertising that either worked, or we thought it did, in newspapers and magazines.

I believe what brought ego into play in our business was the creation of the one hundred percent real estate company concept. Now I am not saying there is anything wrong with that concept; as a matter of fact the broker I was with in the early 1980's suggested I convert to that.

The real estate agent is the one who began the ego age. One of the dictionary's definitions of ego is: selfishness, one who is completely devoted to one's own welfare and interests. It is very interesting to look at words and their definition.

The word advertising may not run smoothly with the other words in the title of this chapter; however it is important you think about it as it can become very costly part of your business.

Personally, I think the cost of advertising has really gotten out of hand. You watch television for thirty minutes and get fifteen or more commercials. And those automobile commercials on the radio are the most outlandish events on the face of the earth! All that yelling and screaming as if to say if you don't get down to the dealership in the next forty seven minutes you are going to miss out on the greatest event of your entire financial history!

Now don't confuse ego with self confidence, and pride in yourself. To me, faith in yourself ranks right up there with faith in God. If you don't think highly of yourself that is the first issue you need to work on and get it started right now, before you even finish this chapter.

I am sure you have seen the words: **ATTITUDE IS EVERYTHING.** The entire idea of this book is to get you to look toward the positives and not the negatives; however it is necessary to recognize reality.

Therefore if the reality is that you are puffing yourself up, spending money on advertising that is not profitable then it is time to make some changes. After all we will not live forever (at least not here on earth,) and since I've gone through many mindsets, patterns, and habits where I have had to make changes, I've realized how great it made me feel.

Remember: YOU are the greatest person there is on the face of the earth. YOU are unique. YOU have unlimited capabilities. YOU can do anything you want to do. You may have a spouse, parents, children, or sweetheart you really think the world of, however if you can't love yourself how can you begin to love someone else?

Take time to write some affirmations such as: "I am a great sales person" "I am honest and grateful to all my clients and customers" "I prospect daily" you think of another five or ten and write them down. These are just as important to have in writing as your short term and long term goals.

Don't get off on the wrong track thinking success is a certain amount of gross commissions, or selling a certain number of homes. **One of the key ingredients to success is happiness.**

If you think selling sixty homes in twelve months is success and you have an associate who sells twenty homes during the same time frame and you give away, discount or adjust your commission down sixty six and two thirds of a percent; guess what? You are working your butt off for nothing!

Please understand ladies and gentlemen I am not a critic. **All I want to do is help you.** Sometimes I may sound like I'm preaching; well I am and it is all for your benefit!

Again, anyone I can help, not make some of the mistakes I have made in the past twenty-five years as a Realtor, or anyone I can help not make some of the mistakes I have not made; that is my goal.

If you don't take care of the customer, someone else will.

Unknown

Chapter Twenty Two

The Pumpkin Man

Myth: Giving away pumpkins is stupid.

Reality: For me it has been one of the greatest experiences I have ever had, I have been able to help put smiles on thousands of children's faces, take away the pain of a parent (if only for a few minutes) while they experience a smile on their son or daughter's face, and all for the simple gift of a pumpkin and the love that goes with it. At the same time I receive more **media coverage at no cost,** in two weeks, than 20,000 Realtors in five years.

This chapter is possibly the most astounding chapter of all. I was wondering how could this possibly benefit the reader, someone wanting to increase their income by $10,000 or $50,000, or someone who has been in the business six months who is a bit disappointed but a burning desire to stay in the real estate sales arena; this could spark some ideas in your mind. I also wondered if it would elicit a few laughs maybe even a tear or two.

I feel you could benefit in several ways. You might find it silly, or it might make you smile. Someone else might get a few laughs, and for some perhaps it will light up that computer between your ears and generate an outlandish idea or two. At any rate, once the wheels start turning you may come up with a marketing idea that will be so creative it will really put you on the map!

Realize that if you execute your idea well, you will be remembered for it long after you have stopped using it.

Ready? Here we go... One year I purchased 250 pumpkins. We rented a little tractor-trailer not much bigger than a riding lawn mower, and my wife drove my son, a friend of his and I, ran around to every home in the neighborhood. I would take a pumpkin off the trailer, pin a business card to the top of the pumpkin, go ring the doorbell (in broad daylight,) put the pumpkin on the doorstep and go grab the next one and head off to the next house. It helps to be in great physical shape (and I was) when you plan on doing something like this for two or three hours!

It was well received. Some people managed to get to the door ready to yell at us for ringing the bell and running, but then they saw the little trailer and the pumpkin at their door; their response quickly changed their attitude to a big:
"THANK YOU!"

The next year we got bigger and better, finding a company to loan a large truck, and we purchased several hundred more pumpkins, and more people became involved. It became sort of a parade, with antique cars, like model A's and model T's. Because we were taking over the city streets of Phoenix, we now needed a parade permit, and in order to get the permit, insurance was required. Topping that, to make everything more exciting and official looking, six motorcycle police officers accompanied us on the parade route. So there I was in a bright orange suit, surrounded by a half dozen Phoenix police officers. Not that any protection was needed. It just made it all look official. I still have a photo of that event.

Not only that, but somehow TV channels 3, 5 10, 12 and 15 all found out about it and came out to do a filming of the event. I still wonder today how they knew, and who could have called them?

A couple more years passed and the event continued to grow. My family and I were vacationing in Hawaii one year and picked up a copy of the newspaper USA TODAY something new to us. Later that year, a real estate broker from California asked to ride in the parade. She said she had mentioned to the passenger next to her on the flight to Phoenix that she was going to be in a pumpkin parade, and he said: "Oh yes, I read it here in USA TODAY, and gave her the copy to bring to me. So here we are, only two years into this and already we have national news coverage. PHOENIX REALTOR, DAN D. McGINNIS who doubles as "THE PUMPKIN MAN" is out delivering pumpkins again, and this year to children in hospitals.

Talk about a barrel of fun, riding in one of three television station helicopters in an orange suit, and green shoes, with 40 pumpkins, landing on the helo pad lined with nurses waiting to load the pumpkins on a gurney and deliver them to the children in their rooms.

The most difficult issue was holding back tears, now I know how Santa Claus feels! The big difference... I was there to see them receive their pumpkin, I actually handed it to them. Whereas Santa Claus can't stick around to see the joy on the children's faces; as he goes to millions where we only do hundreds.

The parade grew larger each year. All year long when I saw something unusual going down the street I would chase it down and ask them to drive their vehicle in the pumpkin parade.

One year a reporter from The Arizona Republic called and asked to come out to our home for more than an hour's interview. Since I had a small pumpkin patch in the back yard it was ideal for a quick photo in my orange suit, as the 2000 pumpkins had not yet arrived for the parade day. A few days later there I was front page of the local section, holding a pumpkin up in each hand with a big smile, and an almost full-page story about "The Pumpkin Man".

I have not made it to Hollywood yet, but I sure know the unbelievable emotion it can bring. A bit overwhelming, when seven year old girls come up and ask for your autograph, and kids send you letters from schools and hospitals thanking you for their pumpkin.

Just to give you a run down of the final years (10 in all,) that this turned into.

We ordered four large helium tanks delivered the night before to our home, oh yes; let me digress a bit here. One of the funniest and neatest entries in the World's Largest Pumpkin Parade was when one of the Phoenix Police Officers brought over three mini patrol cars the night before to store them at our home. This is wild, folks!!!! They were so cute I don't recall ever seeing one before. It is a go cart with a police patrol car body on it, and the top is open so that an adult can get in and drive it with their head sticking out of the roof of the vehicle.

I asked Officer Ron Chicola if I could possibly just take it for a little spin up the street. I got inside, and Ron started it up. By the way, he said, "it also has a switch here to turn on the flashing lights, as well as a siren". I don't recall ever having so much fun in my life! It was dark, I headed east on Yale Street from the 3600 block to 38th Street and south bound to Wilshire. In order to understand the excitement while you are reading this, you need to realize, it is dark, the flashing lights are real, and the siren is real. It is about 8:25 p.m. on a Friday night, in a residential neighborhood made up of people in their 20's to retired people in their 70's not to mention there must have been thirty or more dogs in the neighborhood all barking and howling. Got the picture? Are we having fun or not?

When we arrived back at our house, we all went inside and a few minutes later there is a knock at the door. It was another officer. Can you believe it, someone called in a complaint? As I answered the door, he was about as surprised as I because of course; with me at the door were two Phoenix Police Officers.

He said: "We got a complaint up the street of noise" and my response was: "Officer we are preparing for the World's Largest Pumpkin Parade tomorrow morning at 9:00 a.m. and I was just testing out one of the mini patrol cars". Now here is something I am really proud of: Folks this is called great salesmanship, I asked the officer who had complained, he said "I can't tell you," I asked again, and he said "I can't tell you," I asked again, and I said I just want to know who doesn't like me, that's all I won't hurt him or her, I don't own a gun, I am THE PUMPKIN MAN. <u>And he told me which house it was that called in the complaint!!!!!!</u>

With all the excitement I would get about three hours of sleep, and at 5:00 a.m. past clients, and friends arrived on the front porch to fill 3,000 10 inch balloons with helium, tying 4 ft. strings on each one. Parade entries started arriving around 7:00 a.m. There was the U. S. Navy Aircraft Carrier Float that had come in from San Diego. The Phoenix Cardinal Cheerleaders, a ladder fire truck, The Creighton Middle School Marching Band, North High School Marching Band, a Phoenix Fire Department Engine that had been pulled out of service for the parade, with orange Pumpkin Man helium filled balloons blowing in the wind from the corners of the engine. More than a dozen antique cars, military vehicles, children in costumes riding on floats were also in this parade.

In addition a costume contest with prizes was held in our front yard just before the parade began. I made it a point to quickly designate the judges myself, because the Pumpkin Man is no dummy. They included my broker, an elder from church, a former client, and anyone who I could point to and say "you are a judge," and get myself out of the situation.

OK now on with other parade entries, U. S. Navy, Army, Marine and Air Force ROTC drill teams from schools through out the Phoenix area were there. We made another sale to the color guard of a military school in Salina, Kansas to fly to Phoenix and lead the parade. Since our son was in the color guard I though why not? The Wild Women of the West is a group of women riding horses dressed like they did in 1900 whooping and yelling in their bright colored yellow, green, and red dresses. And the city required pooper scoopers behind every equestrian entry. That my friend, is one of the more difficult sales jobs, finding a couple of boys who would be humiliated in public on a four mile parade route televised on three stations. But you pay someone enough and they will do anything.

Even the Rent-a-Fan Club (something else I helped invent, that got media coverage,) had an entry. I think you get the gist of it. All in all, the World's Largest Residential Pumpkin Parade grew to more than fifty entries.

The police officers blocked off the streets, and maintained control yet they really enjoyed seeing all the fun and excitement people were having. My wife and I rode in a white convertible Rolls Royce someone volunteered. Between the two of us, we managed to throw out 500 pounds of candy along the parade route. We also had a Grand Marshal on a convertible with their signs, and of course the Pumpkin Queen.

Now I will tell you to keep things simple the only way to get a queen and grand marshal is for me to just pick who I wanted in private and say you are it, dress for the occasion and show up on time. And it worked every year. NO ONE ever questioned where or how the queen or grand marshal was chosen.

The final entry was a truck with 2,000 pumpkins and about 10 boys with "Friend of the Pumpkin Man" T shirts, handing out pumpkins.

The parade ended in a nearby shopping mall, where we had a presentation of plaques to all the marching units in the parade, and a pumpkin pie eating contest for kids.

I've had to leave out, I mean a lot of funny events, and a lot of "I can't believe you did that's" however I am sure you get the idea that Christmas was a bit of a let down for me during those ten years of: THE PUMPKIN PARADE.

One last thought, getting to fly of those helicopters in my orange suit with the back seats and floor full of pumpkins was one of the greatest moments of my life. During that time I learned what a 'tease' is in television lingo. Two or three times before and during the news that evening they would show a blip of THE PUMPKIN MAN landing at the hospital, or of me handing a pumpkin to a child in a hospital bed, and they would say: "now stay tuned and we will see THE PUMPKIN MAN at the hospital later in the newscast."

One year I was asked if I would mind going into the burn unit at Maricopa Medical Center. I quickly thought now this could be horrifying but something came over me at the time, and I knew I had to do it. I can truthfully say now after what I saw in that hospital, we have been so greatly blessed. It was very difficult to hold back the tears, but I managed, I realized I was on stage, I was actually performing, I had a television camera on me, and children in hospital beds anxious to see THE PUMPKIN MAN and get their very own pumpkin right there by them in their hospital bed. I will never forget one ten year old boy (and I have it on video from the television news) the public only saw his smile, but he said to me: "I remember you; you came to see me last year."

When you have an escrow fall out, or a buyer you are working with not be loyal to you in the future, come back and read this last paragraph again, and you just may realize you are not as bad off as you think.
The videos bring back unbelievable memories when I watch them.

Keep in mind, I am not suggesting you go out and buy 2,000 pumpkins this October and give them away, I am just sharing an experience I enjoyed for ten years during my real estate career. **By now I am sure you have had some great ideas have popped into mind that can help you make a difference in this world.**

As a matter of fact, the "Return of the Pumpkin Man" is: October 2004. We picked up our new orange suit this week!

Today is a Great Day

Katrinna McGinnis

PART IV

SELLING THE AMERICAN DREAM

For some reason, over the years I have heard real estate agents complain about buyers and I really don't know why. They are **your immediate income,** as long as you do what you should do. Please read the material in these chapters carefully! You will learn it must be a win-win situation for the buyer AND seller. You will also learn how to spend three to eight hours with a buyer and have a fully executed contract, in that time. **AN EXTRA BONUS...** When in a position of multiple offers how you can win 95% of the time. You also will learn how to have more control and work when YOU want to work, under your terms and conditions.

Chapter Twenty Three

Realtors Be More Careful

This is a serious business. We need to stop from time to time and look at what we are doing, saying, and writing as the public will see it, and just as important, our associates will see it.

<u>Is your information on the MLS printout accurate?</u> Have you proofed your words in the remarks? Are the directions correct on how to get to the subject property? To get a better prospective of what we are talking about, stop now, pull up seven MLS printouts and review them closely just to see how many mistakes you can find. Would you be happy and content to pay for a news paper with as many mistakes as you find in the remarks of printouts you find on listings in the MLS?

Oh yes, there are many areas where a Realtor should be careful. I say this because I know! Like driving, sometimes I have shown property during rush hour and realized it is quite different from what I am accustomed to. You have to watch all the other drivers, to not only see you don't hit them but also to see they don't hit you.

Can you imagine having an automobile accident while showing a buyer homes? Especially, if it is your fault. Technically you should call all the sellers and cancel showing their home so you are not messing with other families who are waiting for you. It is more important to call 911 and handle the injuries (if any) and the accident report, however when you let thirty minutes slip by with those details, those three families are waiting on you to arrive at their home. Not that I have ever had an accident, but when the thought of this comes to mind, it helps you stop… and think. "WHAT IF?"

This is a business where if you make one little mistake it can affect the lives of several. Put yourself if this position: You are showing homes to a buyer who lives in the area however you are not real familiar with the area, they want you to list and sell their home for $245,000 and they want to purchase a home with you representing them for $495,000. Consider this, you are showing them homes and going by the directions of the listing agent (which are completely wrong) and you go the wrong way a few times, however you remember your client is familiar with the area and you are not. Do you get the point? So please, Realtors, review those directions when you enter the listing into multiple listing service.

One beautiful late Friday afternoon in April 2004 I took a client to look at homes. We rang the door bell, opened the lock box, and as I entered the home, I could hear music and some lights were on, so just in case someone was home I yelled: "HELLO!" and out came two huge dogs from the kitchen and to greet us in the living room. I stood between the dogs and my buyer, thinking at least I would take the brunt of the bite, I picked up a huge toy and threw it a few feet: "Here nice doggie, want to play?" Fortunately the dogs were confused. No doubt they felt they should attack, however would back off as I talked. They probably wondered: Anyone as handsome and well dressed as this couldn't mean harm to us or the home? It had been a long time since I had experienced fear like this. My arms both felt cold, and I am sure what little hair I have on them was standing straight up. I said to Mr. Anderson: "Do you want to look through?" and his response was "NO" as he backed himself out at the front door.

As we drove away still shook up we read the remarks of the MLS printout: "Friendly dogs in backyard" As we went on to look at the other home that evening, we laughed, however we also recognized it had been a fearful time. I called the listing agent and left a message, suggesting she make changes in her information, in order to avoid someone possibly being bitten.

When your listing goes into escrow, and is pending, please remove it from active and put it in pending. You will save a lot of time for your fellow Realtors, and keep them happy so they will show your listings versus not show them in the future. When it closes escrow and is sold, be sure it is printed in the MLS as sold, so it doesn't show up as expired or cancelled.

No goals, No glory

Unknown

Chapter Twenty Four

Less Time, More Money, Representing Buyers

Myth: Buyers are liars, and they take up your time. You spend days, sometimes even weeks with one client to find them the right home. And then some times they end up buying a home with the help of another Realtor, and you make no money.

Reality: Buyers are **a form of immediate income**. It is all about belief, confidence, and expectations. That's right! Believing we can do what we are about to talk about creates strong evidence. And I guarantee you one thing, if you do not believe you can do it, you are right. We are talking about the time we spend with buyers, and up to now you may have often have spent the time and made zero income. It does not have to be that way!

In 2004 I called a Realtor for feedback and to thank her for showing one of my listings. She spoke with displeasure and said: "I don't understand I have been showing this man homes for six months." I thought to myself, the fellow is interested in her however does not know how to come out and tell her, and she is annoyed with him and does not know how to tell him.

There is a strong need for belief; if you do not believe you can accomplish a successful sale from showing a few homes to a buyer after you have done the preliminary interview, you are right. And my definition of a few is three. Two is a couple, and several are anything over five.

Over the years I have heard of a formula in the real estate business. Are you ready? Here it is:

For every seven people getting into the real estate business, five of them will be out of the business in less than two years. This is a lot of time thrown away in a persons life if you happen to be one of the five. And this is one of the areas that help this formula remain true year after year. Here is how it works: You just got your license, someone calls you and says they want to buy a home, around $160,000. You learned your multiplication tables in school, and still know them today. STOP. Something very important, if you learned your multiplication tables, correctly, remember how you did it, so you review this material just like you did your ABC's and multiplication tables.

So you think 7 x 6 is 42 and 7 x 1 is 7, put the zeros in the right place and you have a commission check of around $11,000, lets say another real estate company has the listing, so you now divide by 2 you have $5,500 you divide that with your broker, now you have around three thousand dollars for three or four hours of work! "Heaven, I'm in Heaven" is the thought going through your mind. We left one person out of the formula, The IRS. **We live in the greatest country on the face of the earth, ONE NATION UNDER GOD,** and if you just happen to look at the coins in your pocket, **In God We Trust.** We have the freedom, to sell real estate, take the family camping, to the movies, eat what we want when we want (whether it is good for our body or not) wear the clothes we choose to purchase and wear, you get the idea. I won't take up your time on the list that goes on and on. A little hint here I learned over twenty years ago NEVER COUNT YOUR COMMISSION until the deed has recorded and the close of escrow has passed.

Don't let that person in your car until you have qualified them. Remember, ASK QUESTIONS, ASK QUESTIONS, ASK QUESTIONS. To be sure they can qualify for a mortgage, or if they are paying cash, where is the cash coming from? If it is from a lawsuit that is not over, they may not have the cash.

Next, you may end up showing them ten homes today, seven tomorrow, four next weekend, and seventeen next week, and you call them and they say: "Oh we are so excited we found the perfect home Tuesday and made a offer on it, we were so fortunate, there was this Realtor who was just about to close up her open house, but she let us look inside, and we want to thank you for all your help, as a matter of fact we want to have you over for dinner in our new home after we close escrow." If you get yourself in this situation just once or twice then you will become one of those five out of seven who don't make it. I have been there a couple of times, fortunately I had only spent an hour or so showing them a couple of homes.

IT IS SIMPLE. Always sit down in your office and ask questions. Remember the last time you met with your doctor, accountant or an attorney? Did they not ask questions? And who is in control when questions are being asked? The one asking the questions! Discuss how you work, ask questions, ask questions, ask questions, then explain the agency relationship form, have them sign it. Ask more questions, explain more about the process, and have them sign a buyer broker agreement, depending upon your broker's procedures and your local and state association rules and regulations. No different than a seller signing a listing contract. Would you market a home without a signed listing contract?

KEY POINT: The more you take from this book and make it a HABIT in your business, the better your odds are for success. Read this material again and again until you have the knowledge and confidence in yourself. Do you think Tiger Woods misses a couple of days of practice? Turn back and read it again. Realize also the numbers say 80% of the people make 20% of the money. Therefore 20% of the people make 80% of the money. Which section do you want to be in? I was just told last week according to NAR statistics that figure is more like 95% – 5% pertaining to real estate agents!

After a conversation with a potential buyer, you will/should know the following: they don't have a lease, or it is up in less than 60 days, or they have their home sold and closed, or their home is in escrow and the appraisal is completed. The buyer has qualified for their home. Ask them if they will be paying cash or getting a mortgage? Think about it. For a person who has $5,500 in a savings account and $1,200 in their checking account and you ask them:

"Will you be paying cash or getting a mortgage?" How have you made them feel? When they say: "Oh I think we will just go ahead and put a mortgage on the home." The next statement you come in with: "Well we'll need to speak with a lender, I can have her call you this morning or would this evening be better?"

Explain the time process, that after finding the right home, we write the offer, if there is no counter offer, we order the termite inspection, home inspection, and appraisal, have a loan application, etc. depending upon the requirements of the state in which you are licensed.

Now ask them what they would like to have in a home, features, location, etc. then…**ask them <u>what they HAVE TO HAVE</u> in a home?**

The next step is the computer search with your buyers sitting on either side of you while you begin the search. Listen to what they say, ask questions. Searching the location, price range, and features that fit <u>their</u> needs (not what you think they need) is as simple as sitting down and eating a meal. Once you have three or four homes that best suit their requirements, call to see that the homes are still available, and call the owners for an appointment to show the homes. **If you use this process most of the time, you can show a person three or four homes and be able to sit down and write an offer.** This process can be handled within two to six hours. I prefer to take the longer period and include lunch in the process. There is no need to let them out of your sight until you have an offer written, signed and an earnest money deposit. If you don't, you may end up showing them twenty to two hundred homes. Wow! Should we go back and read the last page or two again?

Since we are discussing buyers in this chapter and we mentioned earnest money, don't follow in the footsteps of a real estate agent who has been selling for ten years and still gets an earnest money check for $500 or $1000. **Step up to the plate** and get a $3,000 or

$5,000 earnest money check for a $140,000 sales price. Get a $10,000 earnest money check for a $200,000 or more purchase.

Learn to NOT be a duplicate of the average. Anything you can change in the parts you fill in the blanks in your local purchase contract gets the listing agent's attention. Shorten the escrow period by a week or two on your offer, as long as it works for your buyer. Shorten the inspection period by a couple days. **You will learn when you have multiple offers and you are representing the buyer, that these little items can make the difference in your buyer getting the home they want or the other person getting it.**

If there is no God, everything is permissible

Father Karamazor

Chapter Twenty Five
How Long Does It Really Take
(Working With a Buyer)

Myth: Showing homes to a buyer takes two to six weeks.

Reality: From the time you meet a buyer face to face, plan on three to seven hours to interview, show homes, write an offer, go present the offer and have an acceptance. How would YOU feel if I a Realtor, wrote an offer for YOU, and YOU were the buyer, and I faxed it to the listing agent, without, personally going face to face with the seller and listing agent? What if there were multiple offers and you knew that, OR even worse did NOT know that? Would that be ok with you?

Sometimes I wonder where some licensees get their training, if they ever had any training, or does their knowledge come from the experience life has brought them up to now?

Now I have had a couple (I will be the first to admit,) to whom I showed forty or fifty homes to, and wondered that had they been with the best buyer broker agent in the U.S.A. would they have got the job done any quicker?

About 1990 I had a couple in the car and we drove south on the Hwy 51 in Phoenix, Arizona (he was a tooth sucker) if you know what that means, well I didn't know at the time what it meant until we had gone out a couple times to look at homes, and every couple minutes he would give a strong surge of a suck on his teeth and it would sound like a mother kissing her two year old baby. Funny now, however quite annoying then.

He said, with a couple of those squeaky sucks; "I bet you'd like to kick our butts out, wouldn't you?" I was so pleased and surprised at my quick response: "No sir, I have about $100 worth of gasoline invested in you and I can't afford to kick you out." Honest! That is what I said. Well it was not much longer and I wrote an offer for them, was successful in getting it accepted, and the escrow closed a few weeks later.

So to give you some idea of "the numbers", one of those transactions out of every 200 might be OK. (That's to keep you honest!)

Now lets look at another profitable and productive format... something new I did just this week. After talking with the buyer on the telephone, sending them a thank you note, mailing them a dozen reference letters from former buyers and sellers, and a booklet from my title company explaining the purchase process, the next step was to discuss what they wanted in a home in complete detail. Upon ascertaining what they had to have in a home, and what they would like to have in a home, I emailed them 40 properties. The next day they called me with seven they chose to see and I narrowed that down to four homes.

I met with them on Saturday morning at 8:20 a.m. at their home, spent 45 minutes explaining the process of purchasing a home, then we got in the car, looked at the four homes, came to my office, wrote an offer, and contacted the listing agent to present the offer. Total time: five hours 45 minutes. We have an accepted offer.

Another option would be to have the buyer come to your office, counsel with them, and then with the use of the computer, and choose three or four homes to show them. Either way, one of the keys to a successful situation is to go immediately after the offer is written, and get an acceptance from the seller, before there is an opportunity for other offers to come in.

If you write an offer today prior to 6 p.m., you should do everything you can to have an acceptance the same day. NEVER PUT OFF UNTIL TOMORROW to present an offer on another Realtor's listing. Or even your own listing – this allows less time for another agent to write an offer on your listing.

If you have been in the business some time, and you are not handling your transactions with buyers as mentioned above you might strongly consider making some adjustments in your process.

If you are new in the business and have no bad habits in place that are necessary to break, this is the ideal time and ideal format to put into place when working with a buyer. You are not marrying the person, you are simply asking questions, determining what they want, and then finding it. You are helping them accomplish their needs and goals. If they are a serious buyer, they don't want to look at homes for a month and they don't want to look at ten or thirty homes… they have other things to do. And you have other things to do as well, such as find another buyer, find another seller, spend time with your family, go fishing, go shopping, or just sit back on the patio with a glass of ice- cold lemonade and read a good book.

Depending on the state you practice real estate in, and the rules, regulations and procedures; you should have around another five hours to work with this transaction once you had an accepted until close of escrow, depending on whether you have an assistant or a closing coordinator. Therefore, depending on the price of the home and your commission split with your broker, you have in the vicinity of ten hours of time and a commission check of $2,500 to $7,000. Round figures would make that approximately three hundred dollars per hour. Remember – there are a days of possibly not selling & that income comes down to $50.00 - $125.00 less expenses. Always look at net!

Just guessing, I would say that is more money than a school teacher with four years of college makes, or more than many doctors make and more than most attorneys make. Therefore some of the material in this chapter may make the idea of a real estate sales career sound very inviting. And it is, or should I say it is to me, and there has never been a time (even when I was in a valley) in my 25 year career where I wanted to quite and do something else.

This is a very exciting part of the real estate business. You have the opportunity (when working with a buyer) to help someone accomplish their needs and goals, and have a nice check in as little as two to six weeks.
Total investment: less than ten hours of your time. Pretty simple.

You might want to keep in mind, buyers are not for everyone, and the same goes for the other side, listings are not for everyone. **KEY POINT,** If you can't help a buyer with the process and time restraints we have discussed in this chapter, maybe you would be better off to refer your buyer to another one of your associates and collect a referral fee that is something like $1,200 for handing a name and telephone number of a person to another person. Not bad money even for living in this great country of ours.

For myself, I just could never come to the mindset of handing off someone to another agent because I was not able to meet their needs and desires. It is quite common for agents doing larger amounts of production to have what is called a buyers agent, and that person strictly works with all the buyers for that Realtor. Another thought if you do like working with buyers but are having difficulty with other areas of the business, you might consider looking for a position with a Realtor doing a large volume of business (meaning 75/ 100 or more transactions each year,) and see if they will let you work with them handling the needs of the buyers.

By no means would I tell you what to do. This is simply a possible option for that person who enjoys being a sales person in real estate, however might be having a difficult time finding just where they fit in best and enjoy it. **Enjoying what you do has a little more value than money.** It is sort of like: Which is more important? Your health or money? When you look at that question your outlook on things changes quickly.

KEY POINT Never meet a buyer to show a home before having them pre qualified. If they say they are paying cash, ask where the cash is, and where did it come from. If they are not willing to talk with your lender you should not be showing them property. One exception: If they have a conditional loan approval letter from another lender.

Success is a journey, not a destination

Unknown

Chapter Twenty Six

Successful Negotiations Must Be Win-Win

Over the years I have noticed real estate agents (including myself from time to time when I get off track) attempt to be attorneys defending their client, and hammering the other agent and their client. It is like an argument... the "I will fight until I win" argument. And most of the time if you have a mindset, attitude and personality that comes across as abrupt, you will usually loose out in the end.

We need to understand the analogy of win – win. Robert Dennerlein, a client of mine works for the federal government agency of Homeland Security at Sky Harbor International Airport and taught negotiating for ten years with the Phoenix Police Department. He mentioned this concept to me when we were discussing an extremely low offer on their home not long ago that was quite enlightening; he was discussing negotiating with a person who was holding people hostage.

I had never thought of that before, however as he said: "it must be a win – win situation." If I were in that situation, I would not want to give the criminal anything, however I assume you must give them something in order for them to somehow win, in order for the hostage to win and be released.

Asking questions, using alternates of choice and tie downs are quite appropriate when you are in this phase of the transaction. Let's look at some examples:

You are representing the seller. You have an offer from a buyer and the buyer has his own real estate agent. The list price is $190,000 the offer is $188,000. The offer is accepted. However during the inspection period, along with a few other minor items in need of repair totaling less than $400 to fix, it is determined the roof is well over 15 years old and needs to be replaced. The buyer asks for a $5,900 based on two roof estimates. The seller is outraged and refuses. At this time the listing agent politely explains: "If" you were a buyer and in this position wouldn't you feel the roof should be "replaced"? Then we have a response from the seller. Next: "Does it" make sense, the buyer having given us a near full price offer, and is asking for nothing out of the ordinary should have a home with a roof with some life time left in it?

If that still doesn't work and you find out from the buyer's agent the buyer is still very interested in the home, plus and can qualify for an additional $2,000 more, confirming that you feel the home will appraise for $190,000, then suggest: "Why don't we ask the buyer to pay $2,000 more in price and you pay the balance for the roof replacement, does that make sense"?

Ladies and Gentlemen: this is not hocus pocus make up stuff; this is a live situation I am in right now, so it is material and verbiage actually used in real situations.

Let's look at another example: The sale price is $155,000 the buyer offers $156,000 and asks the seller to pay $3,000 of his closing cost. The inspection period comes and the buyer asks for nothing in repairs from the seller. However at the closing table there has been a misunderstanding and you find with the buyer's loan he needs $14,900 more in the form of a down payment than he had expected, and he does not have the money. He rushes to look at every possible resource to see if he can raise or find $15,000 in 24 hours with no success. The listing agent is outraged. The buyer's agent explains the sorrow and apologizes for the mistake, however asks: "My buyer can have the money and close escrow within ten days, will that work for you?" to which the listing agent keeps coming up with: "no," without going to their client and explaining the situation to see if there can be a meeting of the minds.

The buyer's agent then explains, "well you can take the buyer's earnest money of a mere $600 and start looking for another buyer, however the property was on the market 49 days before we came along, and it will take you at least another 45 days to find a buyer, get a loan approved, and close escrow." That is if you have a qualified approved buyer, and the buyer offers as good of a price as this buyer. Or you can extend the close of escrow for ten days and move on. "Does that make sense?" Here again we have a tie down from the selling agent to the listing agent.

Successful negotiating is one of the key issues in successfully listing and selling real estate. You use it in almost all transactions. Yes sometimes you walk in on a listing appointment, suggest a list price of $175,000 and the seller says ok. The home has no need of repairs or staging, you place it on the market, you have two or three showings, and get an offer within a couple of hours or days or weeks in a great market and it is a full price offer. Conversely, the buyer offers maybe $2,000 below the list price, and the seller is tickled to death because they didn't expect a full price offer anyway. However, this is not necessarily a realistic scenario.

Often our problems are caused by our own doing. If you automatically ask the buyer for a $2,500, $5,000 or $10,000 earnest money instead of $500 you can get it. They may need to transfer some funds into their checking account. **Fellow Realtors need to wake up and realize $500 earnest money is what we got 25 years ago.** Gasoline used to cost forty cents a gallon, now it is $1.75 to $3.00 per gallon. You used to buy a piece of candy for a penny now it's five times as high.

Help your sellers understand when they get an offer that is somewhat unexpected and in their mind not realistic, they don't have to counter the offer to the full listed price. Let the buyer feel they have obtained some concession.

Most importantly remember money isn't everything. If the buyer asked if the washer and dryer stay with the property, always answer their question with a question: "did you need a washer and dryer?" Surprisingly, they will often say no. If they say they have no washer and dryer, this may be something you can use if the offer is too low in price, suggest to the seller if we come up $2,500 would you be willing to leave the washer and dryer? Granted, that is an expensive washer and dryer, however it is an effort to help the buyer win and the seller win also.

You must never get emotionally involved. Always remember you have a buyer who in most cases wants the home, and a seller who wants to sell. You have a simple job; find a meeting of the minds so both are happy, you get paid, and don't forget to ALWAYS stay in touch with that client after the close of escrow by mail every two weeks for the next six months, also a phone call a few times to see everything is satisfactory with their home, in order to grow your business.

Hopefully, you will find that 60% to 80% of your business is referred to you from former clients or people who know you do an excellent job of negotiating with clients to have a win – win outcome.

ACHIEVEMENT

...The achievement of your goal is assured the Moment you commit yourself.

Unknown

Chapter Twenty Seven

Buyer's Agent with Multiple Offers

Many real estate agents are not knowledgeable in this area. **From these two chapters on multiple offers, you could earn enough money to pay your children or grand children college tuition! And if you don't already do so (grow up) represent your buyer, properly and physically go meet the seller and listing agent and present your offer in person! It is your fiduciary duty!** Keep in mind what you read here may vary depending on your state department of real estate requirements, rules and regulations, and any of your local board or your company or brokers policies.

In Arizona (currently) if the agent representing the buyer wishes to be present for the presentation of their offer to the seller, they are permitted to do so, unless the seller has requested in writing they not accompany their offer. Well call me old fashioned, or whatever you wish, my feelings are that I have a better idea of what is going on, & what the situation is more so if I am present than if I am not present, and leave it up to the listing agent to present the offer of my buyer.

I will now give you a few examples of ACTUAL EVENTS where I have been involved in representing a buyer recently in order for you to see more clearly what I am talking about, because this is a very important issue. Why...? Because you have worked for hours, possibly days or even weeks to get to the point of writing an offer, and if you don't get an acceptance you have created stress, for you, your buyers, and spent a lot of time to make nothing.

In the early evening a couple of years ago, I drove up in front of a property which I had shown my buyer that day and had made an appointment with the listing agent to meet her there and present a offer to her seller. As I got out of my car the listing agent came across the street and up to the front door of the subject property I was not aware, however she was a Realtor. I assumed this was the seller coming home from visiting her neighbor, or it was a neighbor coming to visit the seller. And then the lady, in house shoes and shorts spoke to me. Two years later, and I still remember that history making night. Ladies and Gentlemen we are in a profession where we are making more than a million dollars a year, or $250,000 or $100,000 or can we say $40,000 per year and we dress like this!?

After presenting a offer within $1,000 of the asking price, the seller was ready to sign, however the lady in the house shoes suggested they have a couple of days to make telephone calls, and be sure they could find a place to store the furniture, as the seller would be renting until their new home which was already under construction, was completed. To which I said NO, accept the offer now. After a few minutes of babbling I told the seller and listing agent, if they would accept my clients offer, I would have the names of three places by 10 a.m. tomorrow where they could store their personal belongings in 30 days when we were going to close escrow. They agreed and the seller signed the offer. And I politely said thank you, and left the lady in her house shoes to get home on her own.

In my market place some ten years ago, Realtors started a habit which became a trend which became common place, and that is just fax the offer to the listing agent. As a matter of fact it is not uncommon for the Realtor to not even have a conversation with the listing agent prior to faxing the offer. I must admit we are living in a changing world, where there is so much new technology changing all the aspects of our lives on this earth. Also…When you are making, or capable of making as much or more money as the President of the United States, a U. S. Senator, or doctor, I feel you are capable of dressing as well as they do, actually in some cases – better.

Some things that can happen if you are not present: The listing agent may have another offer to present, the listing agent may have written an offer themselves personally, for another buyer, and the listing agent may be too over-protective and suggest countering a perfectly good offer. And to make matters worse, your buyer when they see a counter offer the next day, and have "slept on it", could get cold feet.

If you are at the presentation, and there are issues that are not acceptable for the seller, you can assist in suggestions of what to say in a counter offer in order for it to be very acceptable by your buyer.

NOTE: When you go into this position remember you are on stage to perform, don't be overbearing, be complimentary to the seller as to the condition of their home (if it is the truth). You can always find something to compliment the seller on even if it is: "Mr. & Mrs. Lawson I just want to let you know the buyers really like the size of your lot or the size of your home." Speak when it is appropriate, and be quiet when it is best to be quiet.

There are a couple of ways to make things less stressful for you as a buyer's agent and to give you assurance you will win. First of all, hopefully the listing agent has properly informed each Realtor writing offers, that there are multiple offers. It is then just as important that the agents are prompt to advise their buyer there are multiple offers. Sometimes you can quickly determine a buyer wasn't really a buyer, because they were not serious or interested in the property enough to be willing to pay a little more money than they initially expected to pay.

You must have a strong relationship with your buyer, and this relationship begins from the first time you talked with them, so if you met them and showed homes in cut offs, a tee shirt, and tennis shoes with no socks, there is one mark against you. Remember, we talked about how to dress in chapter ten.

Lay all the facts out on the table, and looking at the possibility that comparable sales may not be an issue. If your buyer would do almost anything in order to own that home and if they don't get that home, you have made a big mistake and not only may never see referrals from that client again, or they may slip away and buy a home with another Realtor representing them.

Now let's look at something that will put extra money in your pocket, and have buyers think very highly of you whenever they are in a multiple offer situation with you as their real estate agent. After you have explained the situation to your client and they really want this home and don't want another buyer to take it away from them over a few dollars, tell your client you have the answer to their prayers.

Let's use an example of a list price of $170,000 and there are three offers, one of which is yours. Remember first of all MONEY ISN'T EVERYTHING. It may be a good idea for you to write an offer for your buyer at $171,000 however other offers could be that high or higher if the other buyer's brokers are as knowledgeable as you.

Before we continue to cover this money issue, let's talk about other terms and conditions of the offer you are writing. If possible, get any information you can from the listing agent, (without that Realtor violating agency,) such as the time frame most favorable for the seller to close escrow, and any issues about possession. Don't be asking for the swing set in the back yard to stay unless you know the sellers no longer have any interest in it. An example to make your offer look a little better than the others: Shorten up your inspection period from ten days to five. Where applicable have your buyer paying for termite inspection, home warranty and appraisal instead of asking the seller.

Just a little footnote: in my opinion all buyers should pay for appraisals, it is not the responsibility of the seller, after all if it were not for the buyer getting a mortgage there would be no need for the $300 appraisal. It is time for the buyer to step up to the plate and realize this. And the only way they would feel the seller should pay for an appraisal is strictly because of what a Realtor has told them.

Buyers don't know the process of a transaction; they strictly rely on what we tell them.

Now here is what will make you stand out over other Realtors, even if you are on your fourth transaction, and the others have been in the business five or ten years. Believe me I know, I meet Realtors every month that have been in the business for years and there are things I know that they don't and I win because of it.

<u>Here we go! This is exciting.</u> Carefully explain to your buyer there are multiple offers and determine that they really want the home then explain to them this process. Write two other offers, let's say for $172,000 and $175,000 and then write out a statement for your buyers to sign stating something like this:

We, (your buyers' names) do hereby authorize our Realtor (your name) to represent us and present whatever offers he/she feels necessary in our behalf at his/her complete discretion.

Now asking that other offers be presented first, let's you know what you are competing with, and if it is necessary, allows you to pull out your offer for $172,000 instead of $171,000 or if necessary, pull out the $175,000 offer and present it along with the above statement signed by your buyers.

In my market place, around 1992 Realtors writing offers on other agents listings stopped going to present them to the listing agent and seller face to face, (as I have already mentioned) they just fax them, and are never present for the presentation, and on several occasions I have been present and won over those 'other offers' just because I was there… in person.

With these circumstances and situation I have just explained it is necessary for <u>you to be there in person</u> to do what I have just explained, in order for your buyer to get the home instead of faxing the offer to the listing agent.

Persistence prevails when all else fails

Unknown

PART V

LISTING THE AMERICAN DREAM

Here is what I would call the meat and potatoes. This area is high priority.
This information will assist you in choosing the areas you can get listings.

The truth… about open houses. The explanation of how serious this is and it must accurate material in the MLS and other forms of advertising. Because accuracy is a serious problem with real estate agents! Also some things you actually need to do after you get a signed listing in order to get it sold. Some times in some markets I have seen as much as 37% of listings expire, when that happens you do NOT grow your business and you build a bad reputation.

Chapter Twenty Eight

WHERE YOU GET LISTINGS

Myth: Advertising in the newspaper and magazines as well as open houses is where you get listings.

Reality: The areas mentioned above may be a way of getting listings, however I have not advertised in print since 1995. Many years ago I did advertising in magazines, had a full page ad and it was profitable, even the lottery can be profitable I assume, if you spend enough money.

Most of us as Realtors, should feel an obligation to supply the market place with inventory. It is not good if everyone takes away and never gives back.

Listings are the life blood of the real estate business. They are the inventory in your store. Think about this, have you ever been in a store that is going out of business, and about ninety percent of the merchandise is gone, nothing worth having is left on the shelves and you look at items and think, "I wouldn't take this home if they paid me to take it". Well if you do not have any listings that is what your business is going to look like.

Where do you get that vital inventory? Several areas, so choose the two or three that you prefer. If you try one for a couple months and just despise it, you are not happy, and it is not producing, then quit and test another area.

Myth: With the DO NOT CALL in place by the FTC you can't call people. And if you do call you will get a fine up to $11,000

Reality: In more than 25 years in the real estate business I do not recall any thing hitting so hard as the DO NOT CALL list; it has scared people, made them afraid to pick up the telephone. **There is no need for that fear. You know what FEAR stands for? False Evidence Appearing Real.** We will not go into the rules. There is no need to be concerned that you change your life and your business, because of this new law.

Myth: Calling FOR SALE BY OWNERS is a waste of time. It is too competitive and there are at least thirty other Realtors calling them.

Reality: This is a very good source of business. Why? First of all most of them actually want to sell their home. You should realize you are not the only Realtor calling them. Also many of those Realtors will not call a second or third time, but if you remain persistent with follow-up as well as offering any help you can to the for sale by owner, (FSBO) you have a chance.

 Your goal is to just be polite, helpful, and more professional, than the other twenty five Realtors who are calling. You won't get all of them. Some will decide not to sell. Some will list with your competition, and some will sell themselves. However you can more than make your mortgage payments from the income in this category.

Myth: When calling expired listings the seller is very upset and does not want to talk to a Realtor because they just had a bad experience with a Realtor.

Reality: Don't expect them to be happy, they just had their home listed with a Realtor and it did not sell. So don't expect to get invited to lunch. This is one of the best sources for listing income.

Myth: No need to call cancelled listings, the seller has decided not to sell.

Reality: There is a good chance they were not satisfied with their Realtor and the Realtor was polite enough to cancel the listing and let the seller shop for a salesperson who could help them accomplish their goals, and that is to sell the home.

Myth: Cold calling is a waste of time; these people are not interested in selling.

Reality: Not everyone not even most people, have a Realtor they would call if they were going to sell their home. There are those who do have a friend of a friend, a relative, know someone from church, and know someone from work who is a part-time Realtor. But there are thousands of people who do not have a Realtor in mind should the thought come up to sell and move.

This is such an excellent opportunity for business we have devoted a whole chapter to it in The Hidden Gold Mine, chapter 18.

Myth: You should not solicit business from personal friends, members of church or your neighbors.

Reality: This just may be the number one source for your listings, especially if you are new to the business; you start talking to people in the other areas we have mentioned you will see what we mean, some of those cold calls or FSBO's will tell you "Oh, I am going to list with my aunt, my brother, a member of our church affiliation, a friend, or my neighbor." And there is a very strong bond there. Understand they know that person, even if the person just got their real estate license last week, if they have any enthusiasm and energy at all, that person will be the chosen one.

There are many ways and places to obtain leads of people thinking of selling their home. There are different farming ideas such as:

Geographic farm area (choosing an area) of newer homes, older homes, close to your office, close to your home, an area you like and from that area working 300 to 3,000 homes by mailings, or door hangers, or newsletters on a monthly basis. Highly consider calling them as well. If you are not calling them you are loosing out on business.

Call the title company you do business with to place an order for the telephone numbers in your farm area. There will only be 40% to 65% of the telephone numbers available compared to the number of homes in your farm area, and that is ok.

Other areas you may have already heard of such as farming non owner occupant homes, out of town or out of state owners, repos, former class mates, the list goes on.

Remember you're helping people with their home - not a house, where they will be raising their children and making the biggest decision of their life.

Jeannie Araman

Chapter Twenty Nine

The Listing Presentation

Myth: The listing appointment is a time in which the seller interviews the agent to see if they want to hire them to market their home.

Reality: The listing appointment is an opportunity for the agent to interview the sellers and see if they want to market the property for the seller.

Study chapter 32 as well as this chapter before you go on your next listing appointment. With this information from both chapters you will be in the top ten percent of all real estate agents, when you use it.

A QUICK NOTE BEFORE THE QUICK NOTE PRIOR TO THE LISTING APPOINTMENT:
Here is a very influential statement that can help set you a p a r t from other Realtors in the beginning stages, talking with a seller prior to a listing appointment: "I believe you deserve more for your money, than an ad in the newspaper, a sign in the front yard, and your home stuck in the MLS, that is why I do active and aggressive marketing every day five or six days a week until your homes is sold" When making this statement, DO IT SLOWLY!

QUICK NOTE PRIOR TO THE LISTING APPOINTMENT:
Always complete all paper work possible prior to your appointment. You should always do a comparative market analysis so you can discuss 'market value.' Is just as important that you complete ALL FORMS your local board, association, company, and broker require, before going to your listing appointment. This includes filling out the listing agreement, the beginning date, expiration date, legal description and address of the property,

everything expect the listing price, you may be thinking "Well if I do that and I do not get the listing, I will have used forms that will be thrown away." They will only be thrown away if you do not get the listing.

By completing the forms before the listing appointment there are four key benefits of this HABIT we are creating (1) you get experience in completing the forms and thus become more knowledgeable of them. (2) You have the forms completed on the assumption you are getting the listing, not only do you know this now, your sellers also realize it. (3) You spend less time at the property because you completed paperwork prior to arrival. (4) You will take more listings than had you not completed the forms prior to the appointment.

For the most part, you meet with a surgeon who is going to perform surgery on you, so let's get real serious. The doctor will sit down with you after he or she has asked enough questions and done enough testing to know for certain what the situation is. The doctor then sits down with you and tells you what he will be doing to correct the situation, how long it will take, and what the results will be after the surgery, after 30 days and after three months. Usually after that you have very few, if any questions. You trust the doctor, the surgeon knows what is needed and the surgeon is the one who makes the decisions or at least gives you the options you have. "Does that make sense?" There was one of those "tie downs" I used on you again: Does that make sense? Then the doctor's assistant comes in with forms for you to sign, just like listing a home.

For the listing appointment you need to think in the same scenario as the above paragraph, the only difference, someone wants to sell. They have to sell because of a: (1) Job transfer. (2) Moving up as the home is too small. (3) Moving down the home is too large. (4) Kids have moved back in with parents. (5) Parents are elderly and have moved in with their children. (6) Divorce.

One way to think about this is as follows: YOU are the doctor, the sellers are the patient you need to take x-rays (comparative market analysis), study their blood pressure, heart rate, look at the symptoms (present value of the property,) ask questions to determine their motivation. Ask what their mortgage balances are, present the facts to them. A rather simple and profitable process if you have all the facts, and present the seller with their options.

People want you to be honest. Let me say that a different way so you will remember it: people want you to be honest. The point is if the seller wants to list their property for considerably more than what the value is, simply explain the value and ask them: "If we could get the home sold and closed escrow within the next five to twelve weeks, would that pose a problem?"

I don't like using this statement however I have heard others say: "If you were a buyer and two similar homes were for sale, one for $200,000 and one for $225,000 which one would you buy?" If you feel comfortable with this it is your decision to ask it, and now that I have mentioned it to you, think of a more diplomatic way of making statements like this.

Almost always in my 25 year career I have spent one to two and one half hours on a listing appointment. Every time I did, I left with a signed listing agreement. It is my feeling there is a very large amount of information to cover in the selling of a home, and I feel the client deserves to be told the information, even if some of it will never be an issue for that particular transaction. They will feel more comfortable.

Also it gives the seller the opportunity to see there are a great deal of issues, and that you are thoroughly knowledgeable about the entire process. Also that you are someone they feel confident can handle the job.

Different states, local real estate departments, real estate companies and brokers all have different criteria, and it is vital that you work according to the rules, and regulations they have in place.

Now, after all the paper work is signed, initialed and dated, is when you begin to show how much better you are than most agents. Professionally and politely go through the home and make a very detailed list of any and all items you feel are necessary to make this home show almost perfect. Some agents call this staging. It is quite possible to go through and make the list while you are collecting information and measuring the rooms, however do not discuss the list of recommendations until you have the listing signed.

Some examples of items in a home that should be changed to make it show well:

- Remove the six items off the top of the refrigerator.

- Remove the thirty two magnets and other stuff off the front and sides of the refrigerator.

- Remove any limbs that are touching or within 18 inches of the roof or the home itself.

- Replace the dirty furnace/air conditioner filter.

- Look at a family room which has 15 pieces of furniture in it; ask them to remove five to seven of the items in order for the room to look larger and less cluttered.

- This can apply to other rooms in the home which have too many "things" in them.

- Excessive clutter is unappealing.

- Don't be afraid to tell them to remove the dust off the light bulbs in the bathroom. You know, where those eight bright clear bulbs are.

- Replace any burned out bulbs.

- If they have a practice of taking their shoes off at the front door and leaving them in the entry, and there are 17 pairs of shoes and only four members of the family living at home, have all shoes removed except for four pair.

- Remove clothing, shoes and other clutter from closets; explain to them they should be packed, because they are going to be moving soon. Buyers like to look inside closets, and when they do, you do not want your sellers to have them stuffed full of things they have removed from the rooms. I recall some 10–15 years ago in one closet in a bedroom the seller had and automobile engine. In some cases it might be necessary to have them have a company come in and clean the home. I have heard there is a Realtor in our market place that pays and provides a cleaning crew to come in and clean their listings once the listing agreement is signed prior to showing the property.

If all the windows need to be cleaned, don't be afraid to tell the seller. Check the furnace filter, if it hasn't been changed in two years, it is now time. **Feel comfortable in telling the people:** <u>That the way you live in a home when it is not for sale, and the way you live in a home when it is for sale, are two different things</u>.

Some of these ideas may sound gutsy, however I have never had a person not list their home with me because of this and they always do as I ask. You may feel you can't write this down or make such suggestions to the seller. Well if you want a listing that will sell, and sell for full market value or more, and in a reasonable or short period of time, you must have the attitude and confidence to step up to the plate and tell it "like it is." Remember, it is in their best interest to do so.

Now that you have the listing, mail them a thank you note the next day.

Oh by the way, when they ask: "Do you have open houses?" answer their question with a question: "Did you want an open house?" Most of the time they will, say no… Very interesting… A couple of things get handled responding this way. (1)You find out they don't want an open house and you are not doing something they really don't want, but have not told you. (2) You are letting them assist in the decision-making process of marketing their home. They are involved and you are not second-guessing in your mind that they want me to hold an open house every weekend, when in reality that would be the opposite of what they want!

Finally take a minute now, and think seriously about organizing and planning your listing presentation. Have a friend or spouse video your presentation, watch it several times and find the mistakes. Practice it over and over again, twenty to one hundred times. Your listing presentations in the future will be awesome; **your production will go up, your self-confidence skyrocket!** If you have never considered doing this, think about a professional athlete. Consider the hours a Phil Mickelson practices golf or Randy Johnson of the Arizona Diamondbacks practices his pitching. Now… question…. Do you practice as much as them? If not, why not? It is realistic for you to make as much money as people like this make. **Think on these things.** And I am not trying to beat you up, just help you make major improvements in your business and life.

One last thought…Take a 90 day listing. It will <u>keep you working and honest</u> versus six months! No 30 day listings either. 90 days will keep the seller honest.

The eyes are the window to the soul

Unknown

Chapter Thirty

What Next – Now that the Listing Is Signed

Myth: Input the information in the MLS (multiple listing services) and go get another listing.

Reality: The work has just begun. You got a contract signed and you are now being watched to see how well you perform on stage, in front of a live audience. This is your opportunity to prove you are even better than the seller thought you were when they listened to your presentation. If you do that this will generate referral business.

This is a very exciting time, and may well be the most exciting time of any event you will ever be involved in with as a real estate agent. Some may think the most exciting is getting a check, well you are on your way to a check right here, *as long as you do everything right*. Actually you can even make a mistake or two, (remember you are human,) forget something from time to time and still do quite well as long as you are honest, patient, and focused.

You have just got the listing agreement signed and dated, along with all other documents required by your local board, broker and state associations.

REMEMBER, what I am going to tell you to do now, NEVER do before this point. If the seller asks you "should we remove the peeling paint, should we replace the broken window pane, should we replace the carpet or clean it?" DO NOT ANSWER. A simple response could be: "let me make a note of that and…" Discuss only after the listing is signed.

DO NOT GIVE ADVICE AND ANSWER UNNECESSARY QUESTIONS **until you have a contract signed.** Although the public often looks at us as professionals who know more about the process, and have more knowledge than they themselves do, they are also human, and many people feel they are right when they are wrong, or feel they have the correct ideas when they don't. Thus when you tell them something different from what they are thinking, (it is at that point a little resistance can come in and…) this is where that little nudge of resistance and you may never know it, because they will not necessarily tell you.

Starting in the living room, do a slow and close inspection for any items in need of repair. Go through the entire home inside and outside, make a detailed list of any repairs; sometimes you will find a couple in every home. This displays that you are honest, as well as observant and will improve the price and time frame within which the property will sell.

Ask the seller to make the corrections, and if they are noticeable enough ask them how long it will take them to complete the repairs, and do not install a sign or enter the listing into the MLS until those items have been handled. This will leave you with a very desirable property to have as a listing.

Every so often it is not uncommon for me to have those two days to a week time frame where… I have signed a listing, however it is not in the MLS and there is no sign up. I am just waiting for those final touches to be completed so the property shows well. <u>You can be prospecting for a buyer for the property during this time!</u>

Primarily this book was written with the real estate agent in mind, who has had it a couple of years and is not satisfied with their production, is new, fairly new, just got their license, someone selling five homes a year wanting to sell fifteen or someone selling eighteen homes a year wanting to sell thirty five. It could also be someone who is selling twenty five and needs a closing coordinator to help them have more time off and increase their production.

I don't believe there is ever a day that goes by when I have one listing or six that I don't think about each of them - the home and the sellers go through my mind. Now we come to Sunday. To me this is a day of rest, and one of my days off, unless there is an offer that *must* be presented that day. What ever other time I choose to take off, whether all of a Saturday or a Saturday afternoon, and possibly a couple of afternoons or mornings during the week, these are times when I AM NOT AVAILABLE to answer the telephone. We are all entitled to 'time off.' If necessary turn your pager and cell telephone over to another associate who has set the same high quality standards as your self and if you need to improve those qualities, I sincerely hope this book will help you accomplish that.

Now that we have clarified the above, let me say that during those times you are working, you should have your mind engaged on those current clients, what you are doing, and what you could be doing to get that property sold? Is that seller wondering what is going on? Are they wondering about the comments of the last showing? Are they wondering when you will call again, and when you call will you have an offer? Are they wondering how many contacts you have made by telephone looking for a buyer for their property, or how many Realtors you have personally contacted to talk about their home, or how many mailings you have sent out, and what is the outcome of the mailings?

Put yourself in the shoes of the seller, and if you as a seller have never had those thoughts, realize your sellers... do have. Focus on the needs of your seller.

Are you interested in having a couple of referrals from that seller in the future? Or when things change and in two years they decide to move again unexpectedly, and you are having a slow time (one of those valleys' times) and could really use the business. Keep that possible future scenario, in mind now. <u>It could happen.</u>

One thing is certain. If you do the most outstanding job possible for your seller in marketing their property, communicating with them regularly (even if it is to say nothing has happened since we last talked,) there is a good chance you will get referrals from them in the future. But, if you just do an average or below average job, your chances of getting future referral business from them in the future will be zero! As in none, no more, NEVER again, NADA.

You become what you think about.
Earl Nightengale

Chapter Thirty One

This Area Needs To Be Right

This is one of the most important areas there is for us to talk about, especially if you are listing property, and want some assurance of it generating more than average showings and selling promptly. It is also something I have made it a point of reviewing from time to time over the past 25 years, and some of it is really disturbing, messy, and extremely unprofessional and is costing Realtors and sellers time and money.

You need to realize you are the editor and publisher of information that is going to be read by thousands of people and when you realize this, I feel you will stop, and think about it every time you take a listing. This could mean the difference between selling vs. not selling, or sell in a week vs. sell in three months.

We are talking about the personal remarks you place on your computer print out of your listing in the multiple listing service. This area is an ad to Realtors, words to excite the Realtor to show your listing, instead of one of your competitors. Words to excite the buyer to the point they are expecting 'this is the home for me' before they ever see it.'

Most likely you have an area to show the square footage, types of rooms, room measurements, type of roof, style of construction, what kitchen appliances stay with the property, lot size and so on. Make sure that information is 100% accurate. Now when it comes to the remark lines don't duplicate this information, the agent already has seen it. Give the agent more information in more detail as to the features, proximity to specific shopping, parks, and areas of interest that some Realtors may be unaware of who are not familiar with the immediate area of your listing.

If you have an average size home listed and it is possible a couple would buy it, or it is also possible a couple with children would buy it, keep this in mind when wording your remarks. Don't leave out the single person or the couples needs, desires, and goals and direct your wording to the reasons this home would be ideal for an occupant with two children or with none.

Talk about multiple features, describing a totally remodeled kitchen of a home that is thirty years old is great, however for the potential buyer, who always eats out, visits friends and family at meal time there are other areas of the property that need emphasizing.

Ask your spouse or one of the agents in your office to read over the information, get a second opinion before you make that information public to thousands of Realtors and potential buyers.

A poor example: home features big back yard. Well what is big to you and what is big to someone else can be two different things, and if there are a few people interested in the location, price and other features of your listing however no interest in a big back yard, you have just lost out on a showing and a potential sale of your listing. Let them get there and determine if it is a large or small yard. I am sure you have heard before: Bigger is not necessarily better. For instance to some, bigger may lead them to believe the taxes will be more than they desire to pay. This may very well not be the actual situation.

KEY POINT: When you have an accepted offer on your listing, notify your front desk immediately after getting acceptance signatures. And change the information in the multiple listing computer to pending or under contract that same day. This is a very annoying issue with professional Realtors, this should be ACCURATE INFORMATION. This will also avoid your listing showing up in the statistics as an expired listing instead of sold. With accurate information it is helpful to ALL concerned when preparing a comparative market analysis. It also helps agents from calling what they thought was an expired listing (when prospecting expired listings) when in reality it was a sold property.

Ask yourself: Am I Now Ready To Make Some Changes?

Unknown

Chapter Thirty Two

Open Houses
(What to and not to do)

Myth: Holding open houses will get the home sold quickly.

Reality: Holding an open house will generate activity, or people coming through the home. Not necessarily a sale for the property you are holding open.

A couple of suggestions, if you are going to hold an open house, BE CAREFUL, women and men. Some Realtors lose their lives every few months completely unexpectedly due to some waco out there running around looking to do wrong to another human being. As Realtors we are quite vulnerable. I was told last week, in the past five years 20 Realtors loose their lives each year. When you think about it, possibly more so than any other occupation.

You might want to consider having your spouse, another associate from the office or a friend accompany you. Give them a good book to occupy their mind when you are conversing with someone who comes into the open house. Give them THIS BOOK to read...Why not?

We are not inside a secure cabin as is the pilot of an airline. We are quite often alone with the other person, no friends, relatives or other associates with us. Just think of this from time to time. I do not mean to scare you. Be vigilant and award of your surroundings.

I have heard of those who do quite well holding open houses. In many instances they qualify the person, review their needs, wants, goals and if they are not already committed to another real estate agent it is an excellent opportunity to find buyers, even sellers.

Use at least ten open house signs to direct the person to the property, even if it is easy and simple to get to the home. Put two signs at each intersection as an example. Just pepper the area, the more signs then the more attention, and being different is one of the keys to success. After all there are not too many Col Sanders, Walt Disney's, Abraham Lincoln's or Sam Walton's.

Prior to any open houses make arrangements that the sellers will NOT be present and will not return home until you have left. Turn ALL lights on in the home even if there is not a cloud in the sky. Open all window coverings.

Have a paper sign-in form for people to register. They may seem reluctant at first; but you would feel just as reluctant having a stranger walk in your client's home without knowing anything about them. Have the form pre printed asking for their name, address and telephone number. Many title companies will provide you with this pre printed form.

Introduce yourself by telling them your name, and you have the right at that point to know their name. This way you can call them by name, and find out if they live around the corner and instead of buying, they just may be getting ready to put their home on the market! Wow, never thought of that one. They are not even interested in buying the home you are holding open. It still could be money in your pocket in the future.

Anyone who is a potential buyer or seller should be treated just like that telephone call you made from the office on Monday morning during your lead generation time. Send them a thank you note for visiting the open house, and follow it up within 48 to 72 hours with a telephone call. In doing so you are now a minority, which is great, as most of those out where holding an open house have about the same appearance as a cow in Iowa watching a train go by. That was funny… you can laugh now.

Go well prepared, take a very good book, you may be there as much as over an hour before even one person shows up. Take work with you. Work on mailings when no one is there. It will make that two to four hour time frame pass quickly.

When someone does show up, stop all your reading and work. Show respect to the person, and devote your time to them. ASK QUESTIONS, ASK QUESTIONS, ASK QUESTIONS. Don't be too nosy, however maintain a conversation and help the person with their needs and goals.

You might find out the person wants to sell their home however, and buy another home in an all together different area. Offer your services. That is your job! Don't try to sell the person the listing you are holding open when it does not meet their needs. You wouldn't buy a three legged horse with a one wheel cart, if you were looking for transportation to get you somewhere, would you? If the home you are holding open is a four bedroom with a pool, and you have a couple who wants to downsize to a two or three bedroom home with no pool, communicate to help solve their problem. Don't sell them a home which is like the one they have and that they no longer need or want.

Ideal hours for an open house, Saturday or Sunday afternoons, noon to 4 p.m. or 5 p.m., or anytime you have time on your hands. Understand you will make more contacts by telephone prospecting than you will by waiting for someone to come into your open house.

There are many ways to ask... Learn All of Them!

Unknown

Chapter Thirty Three

Listing Agent with Multiple Offers

This is one of the greatest and most exciting situations to be in as a real estate agent. It is sort of like playing golf and getting a hole in one. This is like July Fourth time. This is an opportunity for you to really show how great you are as a Realtor.

You have a fiduciary obligation to your seller. I have been told my job is to get the seller as much money as possible. And sometimes this can be a very fine tuned situation. In about one out of every 200 transactions when I represent a seller, I have found money is not necessarily their number one concern. Just so you know, people over the age of 75 or 80 years old have less interest in the amount of money they will get compared to time. They do not want to be rushed, they want to take a bit more time to make their decisions, I don't mean go into days or hours, but you might want to spend a few more minutes with an elderly person is helping them make a decision, after all in many cases they have things on their mind, such as they are alone and no longer have their spouse to help make a decision, or, they are having to take care of their spouse as their mate has ill health. They are moving closer to their children, or in with their children, and are wondering if they are making the right decision.

This is about the best position you can be in when it comes to being a Realtor. You have a listing with multiple offers. Your first obligation is look out for your sellers best interest, and next, you are about to get paid if all goes well over the next few weeks, and one of the other agents with offers will get paid. However, there is one or more that will not get paid, but you for sure will get paid. This is your opportunity to review the offers and point out all the negatives and all the positives of each offer to your sellers. Show them the pros and cons however always let your sellers make the decision. It is their home you are selling, not yours.

For years, Realtors writing offers for buyers were sometimes put into a stressful position. Actually everyone involved was put into a stressful situation, as if there were two offers, and the seller found it necessary to counter both offers, the procedure was to send the agents back to see their buyer with a counter offer. At this point the first agent who communicated back to the listing agent first with an acceptance of the counter offer that would be the buyer that got the property.

You know with all the aggressive driving and road rage that we have today, I think this is where it all was initiated... Realtors speeding across town to get to their buyer to get an acceptance of the counter before the other agent accomplished it, and if you go back to before we had cell phones, you can see where it really would have been "the race is on" kind of situation.

This has to cause anxiety for the seller as well wondering which of the two will get an acceptance communicated back to the listing agent first, because you just know the sellers have some sort of preference as to which of the buyers gets their home.

So here is the solution: Multiple Counter Offer. Instead of writing a counter offer you write a multiple counter offer for the six, three or two offers you have. The seller signs them, they are on their way back to the buyers, the time of acceptance is 7 p.m. today or tomorrow, it doesn't matter, however the clause states in this form once multiple counter offers are returned to the seller, the seller then will decide which one they want to accept. There has to be a couple of people who read this and say: "ah ha what a relief."

The great thing in the world is not so much where we stand, as in what direction we are moving.

Oliver Wendell Holmes

PART VI

IN A CLASS ALL BY ITSELF

Here we have just what it says, real estate agents, licensees, and Realtors (those are three of the titles they give us,) you may find this area funny and that is the intent; for those of you NOT experienced in this field, I want to educate you, in order for you to have a better understanding of what really happens and why.

Chapter Thirty Four

Mr. & Mrs. Public... What You Don't Know

Myth: Realtors drive people around all day looking at homes.

Reality: Sometimes a Realtor may not have a buyer in their car for weeks.

- It is often humorous, and interesting, what people say who know nothing about the real estate sales. So we will dedicate this chapter to those of you who are not Realtors but might just like to know the truth.

- Then again, there are a few people who do drive a person around for even months, showing them homes. The reason this happens the Realtor is not educated. Remember I have said it before: ASK QUESTIONS, ASK QUESTIONS, and ASK QUESTIONS. If the person is not ready, willing and able to buy a home, a taxi or other form of public transportation for the buyer, is more profitable for the licensee.

- Realtors do not make all of the money in the world. Although some do quite well, there are those who do not. In 1999 the figure I had received was: the AVERAGE agent sells four homes a year! Although home sales have increased, the number of agents have increased as well, and I feel an honest number would be 95% of all Realtors make 5% of the money therefore that would leave 5% of real estate agents make 95% of the money.

- Realtors ONLY get paid when they have a successful closing, and the definition of a closing is: the deed records.

- No, the broker does not write out checks on Thursday and hand one out to each of the agents in his or her office every Friday.

- Just because there is a sign placed in front of a home does not mean it will sell.

- Just because there was a sale pending or sold sign rider hung under the real estate sign does not mean it will successfully close escrow.

- Sale Pending does not mean the same as sold. Not until the deed records is the property SOLD.

- Just because there is never a sale pending or sold rider placed on the sign in front of the property does not mean it is not pending. Many real estate agents do not place a rider indicating an offer has been accepted until just a few days before closing, in order to make sure things go through. Then too, some agents never place a sold rider on the property, which is fine, it is one way of getting business, someone calls on the sign, and if it is pending they can convert the potential buyer to another home which is available.

- When there is more than one offer from multiple buyers on a property, the listing agent does not get paid multiple times, only once from that transaction, as does the buyer's agent whose offer is accepted.

- Not all Realtors will list a home for the price the seller feels it is worth. Unfortunately many will that is the reason (in some cases) we have seen in the past some 30% to 45% of homes listed do not sell in the initial listing in some real estate markets.

- In most cases the reason a homes does not sell is because of the Realtor. (Realtors reading this… will not like it,) realize, if it does not sell it is the agents fault, as they were unable to convey to the seller the proper price and any conditions that needed to be cleared up for the property to show in A-1 condition. AND if they have the courage to tell the truth to the seller, and the sales skills to show comparable sales, and convince the seller where the price needs to be. This is called "selling" and it is the one area that separates the great agents from the not so great agents.

- The public may wonder why Realtors have their photo placed on a business card along with a picture of their dog, cat, or horse; business was slow that week, and they had nothing else to do. Please don't hold it against all of us. We either didn't apply or were unable to be chosen for Hollywood, so this was the second best attention getting employment we could find. Agents with pets and other odd things in your photo, don't be offended, just want to maintain humor in the book.

- Real estate agents are not attorneys, baby sitters, marriage counselors, landscapers, house cleaners, nor are they capable of solving your misfortunes of money management, and should not be asked to adjust their commission down in order to assist you in your financial issues. When you go to the gasoline pump, you don't get 33 1/3 % off on your purchase because you are experiencing challenges in your finances. Also understand, I am not a mean person, I have helped clients with financial challenges and they appreciated it.

- When you saw your neighbor have a sign placed on the front lawn, and asked them how much they were asking for their home, and they said $176,900, and six months later or next week you see a sold sign and asked them if they got what they wanted and they say yes, it does NOT mean they got $176,900, remember, you asked them if they got what they wanted. Also consider it is possible the buyer & seller negotiated leaving personal property, personal appliances, garden tools, pets or other valuable items as a part of the transaction. These items have value… just as does: money.

- It is not the responsibility of a Realtor to come over and open the lockbox and let you look inside your neighbor's home just because you wonder what it looks like inside, and when you find a Realtor who will, you might think twice before considering using them as your agent to sell your home, or even to purchase one.

- Just because a Realtor drives a Cadillac, BMW, Lexus or a Mercedes doesn't mean it is paid for, or that they even own it, maybe it is rented and their car is in the shop. They may even have a car payment that is higher than your monthly mortgage payment. And if they don't drive a nice car, you might want to ask a few questions… such as is your other car in the garage? How many homes have you sold in the past six months? This one really sounds gutsy but **it will help you,** "tell me WHY we should use you as our Realtor?" Then, **LISTEN CAREFULLY.**

- It really doesn't matter WHY the seller is selling. What really matters is WHY you, the buyer, are buying. At times there may be two, three or even more homes for sale in the same subdivision or even in the same block, and you want to know what is wrong, why are all of these peopling selling. Here is a simple yet realistic example: **Home number one:** the seller is a widow, her husband passed away one and one half years ago and she has now completed the grieving time and is moving closer to her children. **Home number two:** the last of their three children got married or left home for college. The home is 2,800 square feet and they want a smaller home with no pool. **Home number three:** the couple has been arguing and having marital problems for three years. They have finally agreed the only solution is to sell the home and split the equity (if there is any) and move on. **Home number four:** The husband or wife will receive a sizable increase in pay if they accept a transfer in employment and move from Los Angeles to Denver. **Home number five:** the couple had their home on the market last year for $20,000 more than what the market would bear, they are now realistic and have chosen to list it at a price that will cause it to sell and they want to buy a new build. So FIVE HOMES IN SIGHT OF EACH OTHER FOR SALE DOES NOT MEAN IT IS A BAD AREA.

- Most of the time, if a friend, relative, or some acquaintance recommends a real estate agent to you because they have had a great and enjoyable experience the odds of that working for you is pretty good. As an example more than 68% of my business comes from referrals of past clients. The National Association of Realtors has statistics that affirm this as well. And there is no full guarantee, a couple of suggestions: ask the Realtor for references, call those references, ask the Realtor how many homes they have sold in the past six months, in the past year, **and specifically what they intend to do to get your home sold, how often will they contact you by telephone, and/or by email.** Ask them for three reasons you should employ them versus any other Realtor. **This can make a big difference for you to be more knowledgeable and make the RIGHT decision, as a seller.**

- If you have a bad experience with a Realtor that does not mean the Realtor was wrong and you were right. Neither does it mean all Realtors are bad.

- Most real estate agents are kind, considerate and have a family also. They like for you to say "thank you" to them when they have earned it, they don't expect tips for the superb handling of a real estate transaction, and a one or two sentence letter of thanks can pick them up off the floor if they are having a bad year, month or week.

- It is not illegal for a client to provide a gift to their Realtor.

- When you feel a Realtor has violated the law or code of ethics consider taking the proper recourse to have him or her disciplined. Badmouthing them behind their back will accomplish nothing.

- If you are a buyer, the services of a Realtor are of no cost to you, unless you enter into some special agreement (normally called: Buyer Broker Agreement) offering them compensation. However have some consideration for that salesperson. Hopefully, the licensee will explain the process to you, so they are not wasting your time as well as the agent's time.

- It is rude, and inconsiderate to have a Realtor show you homes and not remain loyal to them to finalize the transaction in order for them to be compensated for their time. Not too many people work for nothing. There is nothing free in this world. Please think of this before you have a real estate sales person spend hours with you and then you go off and buy through some other agent. If the person is not listening to what your wants and needs are, explain that to them, and also explain to them if they cannot meet your needs, they need to tell you it is not possible to get what you want for the price you want to pay, or explain to them you will have to find another Realtor who can listen to you and find what you want.

- Appraisers are given a copy of the purchase agreement, prior to appraising the subject property. They go find comparables to justify the price on the offer to purchase.

- There can be thousands of dollars of difference in a conventional, FHA or VA appraisals. Also appraisals for refinancing in many instances will come in much higher than an appraisal attached to an offer to purchase.

- **VERY IMPORTANT IF YOU ARE CONSIDERING SELLING YOUR HOME! Prior to signing a listing agreement, <u>ask these questions</u> in order to have a successful transaction:**

  - **How many homes have you sold in the past 6 months, 12 months, past 3 years and past 5 years? If they have only been licensed six month, it does not mean they are not capable of getting the job done. My first six months in Columbus, Ohio consisted of working 40 hours a week in a warehouse and still sold 12 homes!**
  - **How often will you communicate with me?**
  - **How many people will you talk to <u>EVERY DAY</u> until my home is sold?**

Any questions or comments… go ahead call or email me….

And I hope your day is as good as mine!

<u>Only</u>, in America!
Yesef Manna

NOTES

NOTES

NOTES

ORDER FORM

Order via website:
www.DanMcGinnis.net

Telephone Orders:
602-570-2442

Postal Orders: **Hopewell Publishing**
P.O. Box 71988
Phoenix, Arizona 85050-1017

Billing Address:

Name _____

City _____**State** _____**Zip** _____

Telephone (_____)_____

Email address _____

Shipping Address (If different than above)

Name _____

City _____State _____Zip _____

Telephone (_____)_____

Payment Method:
Check or Money (Please make payable to: Hopewell Publishing)

☐ **Visa**   ☐ **Master Card**   ☐ **Discover**   ☐ **American Express**

Name on Card (Exactly as shown) _____

Card Number:
_____/_____/_____/_____ **Exp Date:** ___/__

Price x Quantity + Tax (8% AZ Res. Only) = **Total**
$24.95 x _____ + _____ = **$**_____

Speaking Engagement Information Also Available